T0256756

New Challenges for Knowledge

New Challenges
for Knowledge

Digital Dynamics to Access and Sharing

Renaud Fabre

In collaboration with

Quentin Messerschmidt-Mariet
Margot Holvoet

WILEY

First published 2016 in Great Britain and the United States by ISTE Ltd and John Wiley & Sons, Inc.

Apart from any fair dealing for the purposes of research or private study, or criticism or review, as permitted under the Copyright, Designs and Patents Act 1988, this publication may only be reproduced, stored or transmitted, in any form or by any means, with the prior permission in writing of the publishers, or in the case of reprographic reproduction in accordance with the terms and licenses issued by the CLA. Enquiries concerning reproduction outside these terms should be sent to the publishers at the undermentioned address:

ISTE Ltd
27-37 St George's Road
London SW19 4EU
UK

www.iste.co.uk

John Wiley & Sons, Inc.
111 River Street
Hoboken, NJ 07030
USA

www.wiley.com

© ISTE Ltd 2016

The rights of Renaud Fabre, Quentin Messerschmidt-Mariet and Margot Holvoet to be identified as the authors of this work have been asserted by them in accordance with the Copyright, Designs and Patents Act 1988.

Library of Congress Control Number: 2016953240

British Library Cataloguing-in-Publication Data
A CIP record for this book is available from the British Library
ISBN 978-1-78630-090-4

Contents

Introduction   xiii

**Part 1. Production: Global Knowledge
and Science in the Digital Era**.   1

Chapter 1. Current Knowledge Dynamics   3

    1.1. Transparency of scientific data   4
        1.1.1. Transparency of access   5
    1.2. Transparency of experimental protocol   6
        1.2.1. For scientists...   6
        1.2.2. And as for citizens   6
    1.3. A necessary form of research engineering.   7
    1.4. Confusion between data and scientific results:
    avoiding manipulation of research results.   8

**Chapter 2. Digital Conditions for
Knowledge Production**   11

    2.1. An economic system oriented toward innovation   11
    2.2. What of knowledge and indeed the
    concept of the commons?   13
    2.3. From analog to digital.   14
    2.4. User–producer: civil society enters the
    knowledge production system   16
        2.4.1. Unauthorized knowledge producers   16
        2.4.2. Promoting "lay expertise" and its necessary
        relationship "with formal expertise"   17

2.5. The interactions between the various spheres
of knowledge production   18
   2.5.1. A form of competition   18
2.6. Collaboration between society and knowledge:
producing authorities should be put into perspective   20

**Chapter 3. The Dual Relationship between
the User and the Developer**   23

3.1. Legal arrangements for knowledge-sharing
using development platforms   23
   3.1.1. Controlled development through Open Access   23
   3.1.2. The emergence of a common market
   for structured research   25
3.2. The user contributes to the creation and
development of content process   25
   3.2.1. The user in the creative process   25
   3.2.2. The user in the development process   26

**Chapter 4. Researchers' Uses and Needs
for Scientific and Technical Information**   29

4.1. The CNRS survey   29
   4.1.1. The 10 CNRS institutes   30
4.2. Diverse uses and dual needs   31
4.3. An explanation through differentiated scientific analysis   33

Chapter 5. New Tools for Knowledge Capture   37

5.1. The growth of metadata exploitation   37
   5.1.1. The growth of the use of metadata   37
5.2. Are we moving toward a semantic Web?   38
   5.2.1. Definition   38
   5.2.2. Web evolution   39
5.3. Tools and limits for metadata processing   39
   5.3.1. Tools being developed   39
   5.3.2. Capturing metadata   40
   5.3.3. Classification of metadata   40
5.4. The challenges of the semantic Web   40
   5.4.1. The main technical difficulties   40
   5.4.2. Data ranking   41

Chapter 6. Modes of Knowledge Sharing and Technologies   43

6.1. Data storage technologies and access
allowing knowledge sharing   43
 6.1.1. Databases.   43
6.2. Exchange platforms and catalogs   44
6.3. Knowledge-processing and digital editions   45

Part 2. Sharing Mechanisms: Knowledge Sharing and the Knowledge-based Economy.   47

Chapter 7. Business Model for Scientific Publication   49

7.1. The current economic model is changing so as to
adapt to new conditions for knowledge sharing   49
 7.1.1. A former model currently under discussion   49
 7.1.2. A model changed drastically by the presence of NICTs   51
7.2. Creation of a new model   51
 7.2.1. Toward a so-called "open process"?.   51
 7.2.2. Moving toward open access.   52
7.3. The issues raised by the creation of a new economic model   52
 7.3.1. Appearance of a digital halo   52
7.4. A new economic model struggling to fine its niche   54

Chapter 8. Actor Strategy: International Scientific Publishing, Services with High Added Value and Research Communities   57

8.1. Publishing, editing and existing: live issues
within the publication of Scientific and
Technical Information (STI)   58
 8.1.1. Publishers' sources of power   58
8.2. Who is subject to it? The other players in
scientific publishing   59
8.3. The characteristics of SMS (Science of
Man and Society)   60
 8.3.1. The national character of SMSs   61
 8.3.2. The specific temporality and profitability of SMSs   61
8.4. Existing without publishing? New STI directions   62
 8.4.1. New STI tools   62
8.5. Alternatives to scientific publishing   63

Chapter 9. New Approaches to Scientific Production   67

9.1. New means of access to scientific production:
innovative models.   67
   9.1.1. In favor of optimizing publication and
scientific collaboration   67
   9.1.2. Moving toward open peer review with
greater transparency and quality   70
9.2. Two main objectives: accelerating knowledge
sharing and promoting scientific collaboration.   71
   9.2.1. Accelerating knowledge sharing   71
   9.2.2. Promoting scientific collaboration:
academic social networks   71
9.3. The need for new analytical tools and the risk
of reprivatization of scientific knowledge.   72
   9.3.1. Increase in data and the weakness
of indicators: the need for new analytical tools   72
   9.3.2. The need for new analytical tools   73
9.4. The absence of the usage doctrine and the risk
of reprivatization of science: the case of social networks   74
   9.4.1. Academic social networks and major publishing
houses: are they undergoing the same struggle?.   74
   9.4.2. The risk of a loss of benchmarks   74

Chapter 10. The Geopolitics of Science   77

10.1. National convergent research models   78
   10.1.1. The United States and sector interpenetration   78
   10.1.2. China: a hybrid model   80
10.2. Science is a source of international cooperation   81
   10.2.1. The European Union: a laboratory
for joint scientific projects   81
10.3. International scientific cooperation is accelerating   84

Chapter 11. Copyright Serving the Market   85

**Part 3. Enhancement Knowledge Rights and
Public Policies in the Wake of Digital Technology**   89

**Chapter 12. Legal Protection of Scientific
Research Results in the Humanities and Social Sciences**   91

12.1. Different legal protections for
different kinds of science   91
12.2. Why protect?   92

12.3. How to protect   93
    12.3.1. French law   93
    12.3.2. Foreign law.   95
    12.3.3. The practical system   97
12.4. Protect against whom?   98
12.5. Changing the challenges of Internet protection   99
12.6. Legal obstacles related to the author's right   100

Chapter 13. Development of Knowledge
and Public Policies   103

13.1. Knowledge enhancement concerns everyone   104
    13.1.1. An issue in the common interest   104
    13.1.2. Multiple actors.   105
13.2. What are the public policies for enhancing knowledge?.   105
    13.2.1. The legal frameworks.   105
    13.2.2. Knowledge enhancement also occurs
    by allocating funding   106
13.3. State establishment of connections between actors:
a key tool in knowledge enhancement.   107
    13.3.1. Incubators   108
    13.3.2. Competitiveness centers   108
13.4. Comparing the United States and the European Union   109
    13.4.1. European Union policy.   109
    13.4.2. American policy   110

Chapter 14. From Author to Enhancer   111

14.1. Enhancing scientific research is a complex process   112
    14.1.1. Knowledge enhancement may take
    several forms depending on the objective pursued   112
    14.1.2. Authors and enhancers are actors in a
    process which is divided into several stages   112
14.2. Scientific research enhancement follows a
legislative framework intended to promote innovation   114
    14.2.1. Public enhancement policies truly came
    into being in the aftermath of the World War II   114
    14.2.2. The State attempts to stimulate technology
    transfers by establishing a specific legislative framework   115

**Chapter 15. The Right to Knowledge: Moving
Toward a Universal Law?**.   117

15.1. Unclear regulatory frameworks   118
    15.1.1. The Internet, a privileged space
    for soft law expression.   118
    15.1.2. Setting up international institutional
    frameworks: the case of data protection   119
15.2. Developing legal frameworks related to
the Internet is complicated.   121
    15.2.1. The historic development of the
    Internet occurred without the support of a
    clear legal framework   121
    15.2.2. Moving toward an extraterritorial
    approach to standards?.   122
15.3. Proposals for developing legal
frameworks for the Internet   123
    15.3.1. Proposals which fall within the
    framework of public or private
    international law or into new approaches.   123
    15.3.2. The absence of Internet territoriality
    and the obstacles to be overcome   125

Chapter 16. Governing by Algorithm.   127

16.1. Statistics that foreshadow algorithms.   128
    16.1.1. The gradual development of statistics   128
    16.1.2. The appearance of automation   129
16.2. Algorithmic governance and democratic opportunities   130
    16.2.1. The importance of algorithms in the
    decision-making process   130
    16.2.2. The democratic importance of algorithms.   131
    16.2.3. Moving toward a State platform   131

Chapter 17. Public Data and Science in e-Government   133

17.1. Disseminating data and disseminating science:
a new requirement   134
    17.1.1. The openness of public data and the
    dissemination of science: a democratic requirement?   134
    17.1.2. An economic and social issue   135
    17.1.3. Protecting personal data   136
17.2. Public data in the e-government   137
17.3. Science within e-government   139

Chapter 18. Surveillance, *Sousveillance*, Improper Capturing   141

18.1. The traditional legal framework for information capture   142
18.1.1. Capture regulated by intellectual property law   142
18.1.2. A legal context ill-suited to open science   143
18.2. The clear need for a specific law   145
18.2.1. What is the legal qualification of APIs?   145
18.2.2. Moving toward the creation of an open science law?   146

Chapter 19. Public Knowledge Policies in the Digital Age   149

19.1. GAFA domination and the oligopolization of the market   150
19.2. Isolated digital ecosystems   152
19.3. Regulation through competition law   153
19.4. Data protection: moving toward a law
for the digital community   154

Chapter 20. The Politics of Creating Artificial Intelligence   157

20.1. History   158
20.1.1. From joy to "the winter of artificial intelligence"   158
20.1.2. A recurrent failure   159
20.1.3. The "spring of artificial intelligence" rediscovered   159
20.2. Artificial intelligence has become a priority
for public and private actors   160
20.2.1. Mass investment from the private sector   160
20.2.2. Smart content   160
20.2.3. Public actors are aware of the importance
of artificial intelligence   161
20.4. The appearance of legal problems   162

Chapter 21. Security Policies in Artificial Intelligence   165

21.1. Security as a comment on machines and data   166
21.1.1. Freedom for machines?   166
21.1.2. How far should we go?   168
21.2. From the security of machines to the security of humans   169
21.2.1. Can machines be made responsible?   170
21.2.2. Data and metadata: where should machines stop?   171

Conclusion 175

Postscript 177

Glossary 179

Bibliography 185

Index 201

Introduction

Nowadays, as in previous times, knowledge is born of out of curiosity, doubt and trial-and-error. However, the process of knowledge management has itself changed profoundly. Due to the Internet, the progress of artificial intelligence, information and communication sciences, information is now more widely shared. Hardly do we start to understand what is happening in this very small community of 2.5 million science publishers, when their results then become both more accessible and better shared by all.

Global sharing, which is a new frontier for knowledge, emerges onto decompartmentalizations never before seen. These involve new ways of doing and seeing things, new logics for "in-depth learning", which are the crosscutting annual theme of Yann Le Cun's course. The latter is this year being held at the Collège de France[1], taking the theme *What is the future position for "intelligent machines"...?*

We may observe that "modern knowledge management issues" are nowadays still partially hidden. However, we can already detect that individual and collective scientific projects are faced with the huge challenges of conception, structure and use. The responses in reaction to these challenges, condition our understanding of the world. Are we actually moving toward a position of greater sharing of knowledge? What are the

---

1 http://www.college-de-france.fr/site/yann-lecun/.

current conditions for such sharing? How is it developing? What is its dynamic?

Regarding these highly evolutionary issues, we have no other ambition than to enable you to share both the fulfillment and interest that we have achieved together as co-authors. As advanced students and lecturers at *SciencesPo*[2], we have "produced meaning" together, owing to the rich and well-known approach of a "Conference" which has taken place over a period of several months. This is very much due to the collective work, which we have compiled from this organic sharing of experiences and knowledge.

Our exploration finds its meaning in a trial of global intelligence of developments taking place. Hence, the deliberate choice of three large spheres to define the "current knowledge-based issues"; production issues, sharing issues and issues regarding the increase in value of knowledge.

In becoming "digital", knowledge production has completely changed over the space of a few years. Everyone has an idea of what this change means for their own use of knowledge. We wished to take a step back when thinking about the conditions for digital knowledge production and review all elements of the so-called production "chain". This involves consideration of what has changed: new stages, new players and new rules. These are therefore as much an opportunity to embark upon a "systemic" analysis of these new value chains. This first stage is obviously necessary for the understanding of the subsequent stage, since it clearly describes "for a given condition of the technology" the various actor organizational models. It is indeed from these constraints and their particular interpretation, that the stakes for both sharing and increased value may be created.

The stakes for knowledge-sharing are vast, complex and dynamic. Their common point is knowledge accessibility. A mirage or a reality? Knowledge-sharing is instantaneous and may take place at a highly reduced

---

2 *SciencesPo* is a *grand école* higher education institution in Paris, whose specialisms include political science.

variable cost and on a very large scale. In the digital era, it is possible to share the conditions for knowledge production, through vast international scientific real-time collaborations, hosted by given platforms. We may also share results, provided that the issues of the sharing economy models and the fair division of value are resolved. Of particular interest is the issue of editorial models, the very old encyclopedic scientific issue, which has been posed, at least since Diderot and his *Lettre sur le commerce des livres*[3]. It is also from there that we may attribute to it the rules and data-sharing arrangements and the multiple profit analyses, indeed also those which we obtain, and even conceal. In addition, there are of course the global and European development of the rules upon this sharing, in the era of "digital laws", and the basis of the new "knowledge economy", which also shapes the modern geopolitics of scientific production.

It is only from there that we can approach the issue of increased value which depends upon the upstream element, and solutions found so as to both produce and share knowledge. Increased value increases our awareness in several directions, in favor of all players. There is increased value of knowledge to the advantage of all users and all beneficiaries of science, through new approaches to open science. This occurs through the organization of controlled innovation capture, in aid of both the economy and industry, through both the broadening and combination of scientific results to meet the needs of society, education, health and social life. These questions make sense in view of the experimentation with new rules, and the law around open science, which is currently in the process of development.

We are obviously aware of the limits of this exercise, which only involved the under-mentioned authors. However, we thought that an overview of these often dispersed issues might make sense. Our justification for producing this collective work is our desire that you might also be persuaded by our arguments.

Astrid ALBERT-ROULHAC

Gautier AMIEL

Jeanne AUSTRY

Hakim BENARBIA

Alain BENSOUSSAN

Louis BERTHELOT

---

3 This translates as "Letter upon the trading of books".

Maxime BUGEAUD

Renaud FABRE

Coline FERRANT

Camille GIRARD-CHANUDET

Arthur GOURVEST

Germain GRAMAIZE

Paul HATTE

Margot HOLVOET

Thibault JOUANNIC

Jean-Samuel LECRIVAIN

Alix MARAVAL

Quentin MESSERSCHMIDT-MARIET

Alix PORNON

Camille ROUSSEAU-LEMARCHAND

Louis SAVATIER

Julie SCHWARTZ

Guillaume THIBAULT

Florence VAIRA

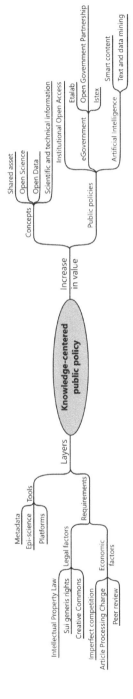

Figure I.1. *Heuristic map for evidence-based policies*

PART 1

Production:
Global Knowledge and
Science in the Digital Era

1

Current Knowledge Dynamics

In his work *L'imaginaire d'Internet* (2001)[1], Patrice Flichy creates the utopian concept of the so-called Republic of Computer Scientists, which is one of the founding myths of the Internet: an organized scientific community which is based upon the wider possibilities for distance knowledge-sharing. This community is structured around four main principles based upon the same ideal of a new scientific community:

– the exchange of ideas and cooperation, first and foremost, which take place between specialists;

– this community is one of equality where everyone is judged by his peers and not within a hierarchical relationship, which excludes authoritative argument;

– cooperation is a central theme;

– it is a world apart, which is separated from the rest of society.

In her statement on 24 January 2013[2], Geneviève Fioraso, then French Minister for Higher Education and Research, stated a second facet of the current dynamics based around sharing and she then declared, "Scientific

1 Patrice Flichy, *L'imaginaire d'Internet*, published by La Découverte 2001 – this translates as *"The Internet Imaginaire"*.
2 Speech by Geneviève Fioraso, *5ᵉ journées de l'Open Access*, 24 January 2013 (a week of Open Access) available at: http://www.enseignementsup-recherche.gouv.fr/cid66992/discours-de-genevieve-fioraso-lors-des-5e-journees-open-access.html.

information is a common resource which should be available for all", thus affirming its will to unlock the circulation of research produced for the benefit of all citizens.

Thus, scientific production is currently in total turmoil. With new information and communication technologies (NICTs), data are able to be shared by the largest number of individuals, without any time storage limit (at least on the face of it). The scientific environment is fundamentally changing with respect to data availability.

In short, knowledge is subject to more general digital developments. It benefits not only from new tools, but is also subject to the same risks.

New knowledge dynamics are structured around three major issues:

– enabling the deepening of individual disciplines and broadening perspectives by creating a synergy of researchers, with national and international projects (and making transdisciplinarity possible);

– providing scientific evidence and also popularizing sciences, which are increasingly now open to "laymen" and other casual observers;

– the research environment is based upon the sharing of scientific data (which allows the comparison and reuse of results). The environment is also based around competition (not only between states, but also at a practical level). In this context, it is incumbent upon national authorities to develop the competitiveness of the research sector.

1.1. Transparency of scientific data

New digital tools make it possible for a larger number of people to access scientific information. Knowledge changes dynamics from two angles. It may be produced by a larger number of individuals, who get involved in its elaboration through the widespread use of digital tools (participative science). However, the knowledge produced becomes more accessible, with scientific data being considered public property, and therefore subject to new knowledge-sharing tools and pooling.

1.1.1. *Transparency of access*

Access to research has for a long time remained both the reality and the privilege of academically recognized scientists. Yet, the Berlin Declaration of 12 July 2004[3] upon Open Access has tended to change this order, by assimilating scientific research into "a universal source of human knowledge and cultural heritage having gained the approval of the scientific Community".

Open Access therefore seems to be the logical continuation of this new principal. It consists of making digital content available, either free from copyright, or subject to the intellectual property law regime. The Internet has made the emergence of such a perception of science possible, through its collaborative concept. The Declaration promotes "an Internet which is a functional tool in the service of global knowledge and human thought base".

The idea is largely to spread science to the entire population, in a democratic manner, and to favor the largest possible sharing of scientific vocations. Knowledge (its production and the consequent access to it) currently exists within a dynamic of democracy in respect of data access.

For example, this ambition occurs by the creation of open archive digital information platforms, responding to very different needs and ideals. *Web of Science*[4], which is a subscription-based private information service around online university publication for the university community, has unveiled a system of online sharing, while maintaining a traditional subscription system intended for an informed audience.

Other platforms display the willingness to provide free services. There is, for example, the *Public Library of Science*[5], an American project with a non-lucrative purpose of providing English-speaking scientific publication with

---

3 Berlin Declaration upon Free Access to Knowledge within the exact sciences, life sciences and human and social sciences. It is available at: http://openaccess.inist.fr/?Declaration-de-Berlin-sur-le-Libre.
4 www.webofknowledge.com.
5 www.plos.org.

open access, operating upon the basis of free licensing, thereby abandoning the concept of paid access. Finally, these projects often draw support from public authorities as is the case with *PERSEE*[6] in France, which is a free scientific web portal for French human and social sciences reviews, created by the *Ministère de l'Éducation Nationale, de l'Enseignement Supérieur et de la Recherche* (the Ministry for National Education, Higher Education and Research – MENESR).

1.2. Transparency of experimental protocol

1.2.1. *For scientists...*

The experiments previously cited all have the common factor of relying upon Internet technologies to offer research interfaces between the various university environments, by sharing results and publications. However, this notion of interface takes on real meaning in the second widespread transparency movement within scientific domains. This is the transparency of the experimental protocol, which enriches scientific contributions from different disciplines, as well as citizens for whom their involvement is no longer conditioned simply by academic acknowledgment.

We then speak of *open science*, the aim of which is to produce and share hypotheses, methods and protocols, which are subject to discussion within a given wider scientific community. The results are freely available on the Internet.

Science therefore relies upon expert collaboration in the domain concerned, but also upon less directly linked disciplines. This type of scientific work allows for greater transdisciplinarity, which turns out to be particularly invaluable in diagnosing new pathologies in, for example, the medical sphere. It also offers greater increased value in research results by increasing the scope of such results considerably.

1.2.2. *And as for citizens*

The idea of participatory science is not strictly confined to scientists, but tends to extend toward citizens who wish to contribute. The concept of

---

6 www.persee.fr.

so-called "Citizen Science" goes back to Alan Irwin in 1995 (with the publication *Citizen Science*)[7]. The idea is that we accumulate knowledge with the help of a large number of individual experiences, especially as far as the environment is concerned. These new data provide a substantial contribution to scientific research by increasing the scope of the experimental territory.

Moreover, in 2013, the European Union produced a report on environmental citizen sciences[8]. This report stated four levels of scientific analysis. These were observation (or so-called "distributed science"), interpretation of data, project design and finally "extreme citizen science", or data collection accompanied by theoretical contributions.

There are thus two major movements that may be observed within this new participatory science: data collection (for example astronomical observations and plant collection) and co-creation (discoveries of new celestial bodies or even PolyMath[9], a website for the demonstration of Mathematical theorems). Michael Nilsen speaks in favor of this latter movement of "networked research"[10], since it not only mobilizes data collection, but also participation in the development of theorems. We may add in this perspective the role played by so-called *Fab Labs*, or "manufacturing" laboratories, which may equally be the breeding ground for scientific experiments carried out by amateurs.

1.3. A necessary form of research engineering

This new opening of scientific data transparency, as well as the broadening of participation, imposes an engineering of systems for the collection and publication of scientific results, which allows data to be used and increased in value.

---

7 Alan Irwin, *Citizen Science: A Study of People, Expertise and Sustainable Development*, Psychology Press, 1995.

8 Report by the "science and governance" group of experts to the European Commission, *Taking European Knowledge Society Seriously*, 2007.

9 www.polymathprojects.org

10 Michael Nielsen, *Reinventing Discovery: the Era of Networked Science*, Princeton University Press, 2011.

Thus, Scientific and Technical Information (STI) brings together information which professionals working in research, teaching or industry may need. This concept, which first appeared in the 1960s, is linked to the development of information technologies and communication. It emanates from the idea that the marked increase in university and scientific output, as well as the profusion of data, necessitates precise organization to optimize such data dissemination. This is, to some extent, a form of knowledge management.

The STI indiscriminately covers all scientific and technical sectors and assumes various aspects. These include scientific articles, journals, copyright notices, bibliographical databases, open archives and accessible Internet data storage warehouses and particular portals.

It chiefly sets three tasks. These are to increase the value of French scientific output in both the European and international arena and strengthen its notoriety, equipping French research with the means for efficient information to develop scientific output and access to it, and favoring information control.

Despite all of the progress and enthusiasm aroused by these new research practices, the persistence of the former publishing practices and the risks of a poorly controlled science transparency confirms a transition situation, in which new dynamics are gradually asserted.

1.4. Confusion between data and scientific results: avoiding manipulation of research results

Within the co-construction of the scientific protocols movement, a single question crops up. Does science strictly coincide with data production? Even if everyone was in a position to produce data, and had the tools available to process it, would its interpretation be accessible to everyone? The resurgence of the split between those initiated in the domain and laymen is at stake. Especially since the transparency of the scientific protocol increases the risk of fraud (for example counterfeits, forgery and plagiarism). Such a risk imposes quality control regimes upon the knowledge produced. In addition, we are witnessing a risk of the spread of pseudo-scientific politically orientated theories. These arise from studies which have not got the necessary scientific guarantees but which, however, crop up as a result of academically acknowledged research.

Moreover, the algorithms of integrated data may insert a form of reasoning bias within digital archives, by offering content which turns out to be pertinent to criteria for word repetition or content similarity. Human intelligence should therefore remain at the center of the scientific process, which is no longer systematically guaranteed.

Finally, the overabundance of data may put the brakes on the creation of pertinent resources. Only 10% of research data are actually used at the time of publication, while the rest are stored for potential future use. Yet, a marked increase in data collected imposes wide-ranging technical administration. We are speaking here of knowledge engineering. However, this engineering may of course apply, first and foremost, to the excesses of data production.

Scientists are therefore concerned to ensure a rigorous framework for methods employed, to confirm contributions or at least institute validation procedures. Although citizens may increasingly be workers producing scientific output, the role of the global architecture must remain fundamentally devolved to scientists.

To conclude, current knowledge dynamics are characterized by:

– pooling and centralizing scientific data with a view to better dissemination, with the latter remaining dependent upon the system of contracts and the scientific publication markets;

– the marked, indeed exponential, increase in data used for research, which are not, for all that, systematically sources of knowledge;

– the transparency of scientific protocol which outlines the contours of collaborative or citizen science but which does not evade the need for scientific expertise, and in fact poses the issue of intellectual property.

It might be pertinent to carry out the same introspection which was conducted by literary theorists as to the pertinence of keeping the author of a work as a form of unshakable institution, summarizing the words of Samuel Beckett, and Michel Foucault thus wondering, "What matter who's speaking?" (*Dits et Ecrits*)[11] to reconsider the pertinence of enunciated authority. In short, should science "become anonymised"? Should it give up authoritative argument and academically acknowledged expertise in favor of stepping over a new threshold?

---

11 This translates as "The spoken and written word".

2

Digital Conditions for Knowledge Production

Digital technologies are resulting in a new form of knowledge processing.

2.1. An economic system oriented toward innovation

The 19th Century was that of industrial capitalism, hinging upon inequality of ownership and access to means of production according to the Marxist analysis. However, at the end of the 20th Century, a new form of economics emerged, the raw material for which had never been contemplated up to that point. This was constituted by innovation in all domains and all forms within science and technology.

Within all domains, investing in research has thus become imperative (see Figure 1.1). This is a subject upon which the G7 countries and large divergent economies compete, as the growing number of scientific and technical articles produced in countries such as China and Russia show[1].

Likewise, sites such as *Internet Archive*[2], *Google Books*[3] or even *Wikipedia*, the famous encyclopedia, with more than 5,000 voluntary

1 *UNESCO Science Report: Towards 2030*, giving data and figures: Publications, UNESCO. URL: http://fr.unesco.org/node/252295.
2 An Internet site created in 1996 with the goal of constituting free access digital archives, bringing together all documents (whether text, images, audio and video material or similar items) presented through to the current day on the Internet.
3 Inspired by major digital book projects such as *Project Gutenberg*, *Google Books*, which originated in 2002, brings together to this day the largest textual compilation work in the world.

contributors have become essential tools, through the knowledge which they make available. This accessibility of digital equipment to the entire population opens up knowledge production to a wide diversity of players ranging from the highest qualified researchers to the most uninitiated contributors.

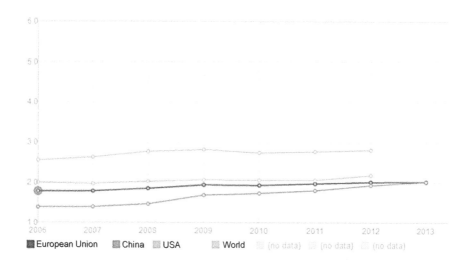

Figure 2.1. *Percentage of GDP invested in Research and Development within the EU, China, the United States and throughout the world between 2005 and 2013 (World Bank Data)[4]*

In a legitimate way, this shift in resource redistribution has given new vigor to old ideals: Michael Hardt and Antonio Negri in their book *Multitude. War and Democracy in the Age of Empire* (Éditions Exils, 2000) say in this new configuration of economics where everybody and yet simultaneously nobody appears to have the means of production, a "mass intellectualism" is formed. The concept "immaterial labor" may thus, for them, question the current system of ownership.

The site not only makes available more than fifteen million books digitized by Google, but also offers both research and indexing services, with complex content, due to the algorithm PageRank.

4 *"Données", Dépenses en Recherche et Développement (%PIB)*, La Banque Mondiale. This translates as 'Data', Expenses for Research and Development (%GDP), The World Bank. URL: http://donnees.banquemondiale.org/indicateur/GB.XPD.RSDV.GD.ZS/countries/A5-A4-EU-CN-US-L7-1W?display=graph.

2.2. What of knowledge and indeed the concept of the commons?

Knowledge has the characteristics of the commons. These two facets are not rivals as such. That is to say that they are limitless and mobilized by an infinite number of individuals, both simultaneously and non-exclusively. Their immateriality seems, on the surface, to prevent them being subject to any form of private ownership. Thus, communities of amateur scientists (or even, for example, those in the fields of books, cinema, video games, cooking and others) take advantage of Web 2.0 and its mine of information to create thematic platforms, exchange or even collectively create content.

These types of scientific knowledge collaborative production or narratives (examples being reviews upon beauty or happiness) emerge together with previously existing authorities, which increasingly shut down access to the knowledge which they produce or capture – due to intellectual property rights. This is because the notion of the commons seems incompatible with a neo-liberal market. Knowledge is thus locked away, protected as it is via laws or patents constituting ownership by those seeking to appropriate them, whether in a just or improper way.

The commons may well be "commoditized" but they should still remain accessible to the entire community. Thus, a movement favoring the commons is deployed. This was started, in particular, by the holder of the Nobel Prize for Economics, Elinor Ostrom. She was the author of *Governing the Commons* which thus sought a "valid theory on an empirical basis of forms of self-organization and self-governance in collective action"[5]. Such forms allow the sustainable existence of the commons between all extremes of state and market[6].

In an article intended to hail the works of the economist, the lecturer–researcher Hervé Le Crosnier approves the idea of both management and different perceptions of ownership of knowledge, allowing "humans to

---

5 De Boeck, 2010, page 40.
6 Jean–Marie Harribey, "Le Bien Commun est une Construction Sociale. Apports et Limites d'Elinor Ostrom", *L'Économie* Politique 2011/1 (no. 49), pp. 98–112 (this translates as "'Commons as a social construct: Contributions and Limitations of Elinor Ostrom's theory").

develop their production modes together and to find rules which do not resemble the market image to self-govern their joint actions"[7].

For fairer power-sharing within society, taking back the commons is necessary, while the converse action may serve the ends of the traditional knowledge production authorities.

Digital uses overturn the rules of economics, society and law. Practices and specialist expertise in knowledge production were modified by the use of digital tools. Moreover, the latter allowed civil society to enter into a knowledge production-based system. Figure 2.2 illustrates the entering of civil society in the system.

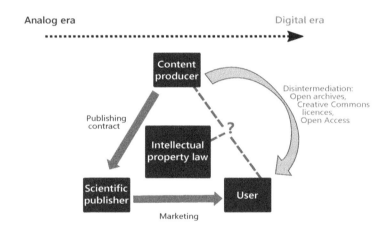

Figure 2.2. *Calling into question economic and legal models for knowledge production in the digital era*

2.3. From analog to digital

The circulation of knowledge has largely been facilitated by the passage to digital. As Eric Scherer explains in his glossary upon the digital

7 Hervé Le Crosnier, "Une Bonne Nouvelle pour la Théorie des Biens Communs", *Vacarme 3/2011* (No. 56), pp. 92–94 (this translates as "Welcome News for the Commons Theory"); www.cairn.info/revue-vacarme-2011-3-page-92.htm, DOI: 10.3917/vaca.056.0092.

revolution[8] "Analog has a physical cost which favors rarity and digital has a marginal cost, of almost nil, thus favoring abundance and ubiquitousness".

In this hitherto unseen context, researchers are seeing their capacity for knowledge production increase 10-fold. If their production rests, in the first place upon the manipulation of pre-existing knowledge, it must respond to the requirements for validity and originality. These criteria are checked under the supervision of other researchers (peers), according to the process of peer review. The need for the latter has stimulated the creation of leading scientific reviews.

Digital technology has therefore revolutionized knowledge production conditions. It has done so by making tools available to researchers which drastically reduce research and experiment time (e.g. information resources, simulation and modeling software and other means). In addition, it has allowed researchers to create more extensive and complex social networks than was previously the case. This communication advantage has become central to research domains, such as economics, not only for the time saved but also the contributions to collaborative work, which proves to be much more fruitful.

Its growing importance makes it possible to question capitalist and institutional models, and increasingly drives us to rethink our ways of thinking about society and, in particular, the drafting of laws. We may take the example of Axelle Lemaire, the Secretary of State for Digital's initiative, hitherto unseen in France. This allowed citizens to directly participate in the bill "Advocating a Digital Republic".

Thus, there are numerous changes forecast for the horizon of our democracies. However, how are research centers, universities and companies (knowledge producers and processors) managing this change? Naturally, all parties wish to avert abuse through unfair competition, asserting intellectual property rights acquired in the 18th and 19th Centuries. Knowledge therefore takes on a private dimension and copyright-protected by means of

---

8 Éric Scherer, *"Analogique"*, *"Numérique" La Révolution Numérique, Glossaire*, Dalloz, 2009, page 224 (this translates as 'From "Analog" to "Digital", Glossary upon the Digital Revolution').

the national and international legislation. This establishes the boundary between the commons and private property.

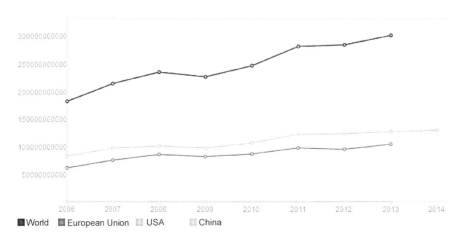

Figure 2.3. *Royalties for the use of intellectual property, recovered (in $US) from the EU, the United States, China and the world between 2006 and 2013 (World Bank Data)[9]*

2.4. User–producer: civil society enters the knowledge production system

2.4.1. *Unauthorized knowledge producers*

2.4.1.1. *Collaborative production networks*

Web resources, our e-mail boxes or social networks are tools which are particularly adapted to information exchanges which go beyond being simply private exchanges. Facebook, Twitter and a great many other platforms serve as windows for the dissemination of laymen's articles, whether they be film reviews, make-up tutorials or messages to raise public awareness of the environment and other causes.

Within the science domain, communities are being created online, arising from the need to share resources, facilitating related exchanges, indeed even

9 Data and graph extracted from the World Bank website, http://donnees. banquemondiale.org/indicateur/BX.GSR.ROYL.CD/countries/1W-EU-US-CN?display=graph.

to study certain phenomena simultaneously. Mélanie Dulong de Rosnay[10] speaks very highly of the advent of these collaborative knowledge production networks. She maintains that, like Wikipedia, they make it possible to coordinate projects in a highly structured way, according to intellectual property law (for example free licenses for Wikipedia). and through modes of governance. Such rules and modes can thus be defined by the individual communities themselves. These are generally based upon a significant level of horizontality.

The system rests upon self-regulation. A study by the review *Nature* even considers that *Wikipedia* may be as reliable as other subscription encyclopedias, such as *Britannica*[11]. In this way, voluntary collaboration may compete with the work of profit-making organizations. However, for all that, is it possible that it might function independently of formal scholarly institutions? Likewise, might these institutions pour scorn upon these information banks being fed in a spontaneous way?

Beyond technical and medical sciences, on these forums, public opinion is created. Multiple actors, such as research firms, businesses and also governments, all face the issue of "lay expertise".

2.4.2. Promoting "lay expertise" and its necessary relationship "with formal expertise"

The case of the platform *Tela Botanica*[12] is, alongside *Wikipedia*, a particularly pertinent example to justify the capacity for knowledge

10 Mélanie Dulong de Rosnay, "Les Réseaux de Production Collaborative de connaissances" taken from Éric Letonturier, Les réseaux, CNRS Editions, pp. *141–146, 2012, Les Essentiels d'Hermès* (this translates as "'Networks for Collaborative Knowledge Production"), https://hal.archives-ouvertes.fr/halshs-00726963v2/document/.
11 *Nature* vol. 438, pp. 900–901, published online on 14th December 2005, http://www.nature.com/nature/journal/v438/ n7070/full/438900a.html.
12 Lorna Heaton *et al.*, "La Réactualisation de la Contribution des Amateurs à la Botanique." *Le collectif en ligne Tela Botanica", Terrains & travaux 2011/1* (no. 18), p. 155-173 (this translates as "Updating the contribution of amateurs to botany"), http://www. cairn.info/revue-terrains-et-travaux-2011-1-page-155.htm.

production by accumulation, or even through so-called "crowdsourcing". Indeed, the scientific community revels in the involvement of amateurs who contribute to the formation of genuine databases by compiling diverse information (whether upon photography, plant location and other subjects). Furthermore, valuable knowledge is contributed which is, above all, non-scientific.

The founding charter of this network had bet upon the invitation of these external players to formal scholarly circles, focusing, above all, upon their passion: "The vocation of [the network] is not to simply produce by itself, but to pool information which its members produce. Its aim is also to make it possible for its members to produce and reflect together. Its efficiency largely therefore rests upon its capacity to connect its members, and to circulate everything that can be circulated, whether information, consideration, resources and individuals. This structuring as a network, is based in principle upon non-competition between the actions of members. It is done by pooling its skills by helping others and pushing [each individual and] the entire group forward towards a common goal."

Thus, the collaborative platform tends toward suppressing the symbolic authority afforded to the knowledge production infrastructure. Effectively, the assertion of legitimate knowledge production forums leads to marginalizing popular science and amateurs, who make a significant contribution. Botany lends itself particularly well to this system, as it requires more observation than expertise, which partly explains the growing interest in it.

2.5. The interactions between the various spheres of knowledge production

2.5.1. *A form of competition*

It still remains difficult to conceive the production of scientific knowledge by non-scientists for reasons of objectivity, ethics and truth, which are characteristics of the sciences. However, web users find themselves in conditions which are particularly satisfying for the production of so-called "narrative knowledge".

In his article "Quel Impact les Technologies ont-elles sur la Production et la Diffusion des Connaissances?", Daniel Pareya[13] explains that "relevant terms falling within the knowledge narrative find their validation – indeed their acceptance – in the fact of being reported, repeated and reaffirmed within a social community, which constitute the forum of legitimization".

Thus, in many respects, we may see in the proliferation of surfers finding expression by competing, in some way, with authorities carrying both information and influence as regards aesthetic taste, lifestyle or even knowledge transmission. Nowadays, what could possibly be easier than creating a blog or self-publishing? How could we possibly now envisage today the promotion of an event or an individual without Re-tweets, or without Facebook "Likes"? Thus, bloggers, whether male or female, may compete for author legitimacy by writing upon recruitment specifics within given occupational sectors, as leader writers or in cultural reviews.

Businesses are already seizing these common key figures, who know how to exert influence over Internet users' judgment. Their knowledge production narrative is therefore used to promote new products, films, books, not forgetting, of course, those inescapable video games (which mention, for example, tweets).

Literary knowledge narratives, previously reserved for the cultural and media elites, henceforth seem to be accessible to all. This new frame of mind introduced by users seriously calls into question knowledge authorities which, if they deny them, risk abandonment or failure. It is hardly surprising that our era's watchword is "Uberisation", in which everyone tailors and progressively develops their practices, aesthetic choices or even their politics.

---

13 For a discussion of narrative knowledge production, see Peraya Daniel, "Quel Impact les Technologies ont-elles sur la Production et la Diffusion des Connaissances?" *Questions de Communication/2012* (no. 21), pp. 89–106 (this translates as "'What impact do technologies have on the production and spread of knowledge"), www.cairn.info/revue-questions-de-communication-2012-page-89.htm DOI: 10.4000/questionsdecommunication.6590.

2.6. Collaboration between society and knowledge: producing authorities should be put into perspective

Are we moving toward an entirely "Open" future, where the users and producers of knowledge might collaborate, or even be the same people? However, we need to put into perspective the share of these user–producers on the Web: making a contribution assumes that given citizens are informed in certain fields, and especially the trend for voluntary participation.

For example, the national consultation on Axelle Lemaire's bill which opened on 26th September and closed on 18 October 2015 gathered 21,411 participants, according to the Internet site www.republique-numerique.fr. Statistically, this is only 3% of the French population. Even with a promising start, the ideal of the self-sufficient digital citizen is a concept to be handled with care.

In addition, in the light of the disproportionate amount of information published online, the Web abounds with misinformation. Major knowledge production authorities therefore remain the most accurate. This is especially so in the eyes of teaching staff among whom there is still a relatively low acceptance of bibliographies without any evidence of paper-based publication and who refuse, for the most part, all references to *Wikipedia*.

For all that, our research of printed sources henceforth comes exclusively from search engines. However Google, as with the largest scientific publishers, categorizes the relevance of works according to the number of times they are quoted.

Although, as Jean-François Lyotard says of it, "a scientific statement draws no validity from what is reported"[14] at which we may worry about a general confusion between truth and consensus. It is therefore more than ever necessary to form and have to hand analytical tools if we wish, as sciences demand, to demonstrate objectivity.

---

14 Jean–François Lyotard, *La Condition Post-moderne*, Les Editions de Minuit, 1979 (this translates as "The Postmodern Condition").

However, the influence of civil society (made up of networks) around knowledge production by the current authorities is unquestionable. The organization of massive social movements due to the Internet, or quite simply unrest around a social issue, may trigger knowledge production on a given subject, by engaging the state in the elaboration of a given public policy, for example, or by stimulating research regarding a health controversy. However, digital technology is not the cause of such initiatives which in fact predate it.

The impact of digital technology on knowledge production conditions is therefore not, in the meantime, a remedy for social divide. Rather, we might say that the gap between civil society and markets has widened owing to ever more barriers to accessing knowledge. These include patents, ever extended royalties and the organization of scientific reviews, which are all too often both absurd and expensive.

For all that, laws in general and, French laws in particular, prevent, for example, the relaxing of royalties by granting scientific publishers a period of embargo. During this period, they may oppose any placement of an article by one of its authors in an open archive. Alternatively, the author is compelled to pay so that his article is accessible to all from the date of publication. There is an entire package of measures which contribute to the rigidity of royalties, this being to the detriment of the creator who would otherwise be entitled to capitalize such sums. However, it works to the advantage of those publishing the article. In this regard, we may see that fair remuneration of the publisher, which evidently is vital, cannot be reasonably determined by the downtime for scientific results to the said publisher's exclusive and prior benefit. It would be necessary, without doubt, to review the basis of this payment so that it is fair and not in conflict with the needs for global dissemination of scientific results.

In addition, digital technology has not ruled out the need for infrastructures among the conditions for knowledge production. Admittedly, positive externalities may be drawn from the activity of Google, with its vast digital book business, or even philanthropic projects providing free access to resources. However, it remains the case that given populations need both equipment and also the ability to appropriately decrypt the amount of Internet information available.

Finally, digital has made it possible to bring the notion of the commons to the center of the debate by involving the concept, to the chagrin of large traditional companies at the heart of a new and growing form of economics. Citizen collaboration platforms, businesses in the digital sphere and governments, must present a united front to lawyers. In this way, they will be able to initiate the redefinition of intellectual property rights, with the greatest respect possible for the new practices we have now adopted. Increasingly, it is evident to some or indeed totally imperceptible for others, that the conditions for knowledge production are in the process of being altered in favor of more openness with the processes of Open Access, Open Science and Open Innovation which are now under way.

The Dual Relationship between
the User and the Developer

New technologies have revolutionized the relationships between the various research and innovation actors, in particular that between the developer and potential research user. This includes all professionals working within IST (the Information Society Technology field) but also individuals and, to a certain extent, the companies concerned.

In this way, the legal arrangements for developer data use and sharing have themselves evolved, as has the role of the user as such. This is a role, which is increasingly contributory and transformative, within the development and content creation process. This generates new problems in terms of formal acknowledgment and legal contracting with respect to this contribution. What are the new forms of contract – or the contracts which exist between the information developer and the user – and how do they revise both players' positions?

3.1. Legal arrangements for knowledge-sharing using development platforms

3.1.1. *Controlled development through Open Access*

Although some consensus in the discussion may be noted, from CNRS and the government in particular, which goes in the direction of the development of open access in Western countries, there are debates as to choosing between the so-called "green" and "gold" open access. On the one hand, there is "green" open access, or self–archiving (carried out by researchers, in open archives belonging to institutions). This, as of now, constitutes the bulk, when viewed in terms of publication quantity. In France, it has benefitted from government support from the Minister for Higher Education and Research, Geneviève Fioraso.

On the other hand, there has been significant vocal support defending "gold" open access, which has the advantage of offering open access to articles on the publisher's website, without a period of embargo. The user may find such articles in their published and formatted version. In short, these are works which are more enjoyable to read with free access on platforms, which are easier to use. This form of access is more restrictive and costly, that is more difficult to manage depending, as it does, upon a pluralism of actors and practices, which are fairly diverse according to given disciplines.

"Green" open access may appear more restrictive in terms of the dissemination of knowledge, development and the quality of service provided to the user. It does, however, have the advantage of being directly managed by scientific communities and for their advantage. In principle, "green" open access should remain the least costly (being non-paying author access), although there are transition attempts (for example so-called "breakwater reviews"). However, although the open access revolution is proving to be radical, the overall consensus on feasibility is developing fairly slowly.

It is important to note that behind the term "open access", whether it is "green" or "gold", hides a regulation strategy (which is certainly audacious, as it allows more liberty with the aim of avoiding infringements). It is a regulation strategy which is both managed and permissible, that, in principle, will take on an increasingly macro and political character, as in the United States. Indeed, in 2013, Congress voted in a law which imposed the principles of open access upon all works financed by public money and the government spearheaded a policy to promote the use of highly proactive Creative Commons licenses, in particular by universities.

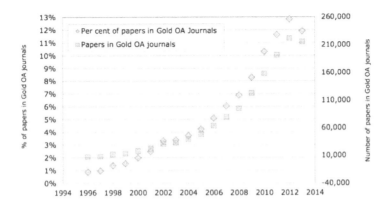

Figure 3.1. *Growth of Gold Open Access between
1996 and 2014 (per Archambault – 2014)*[1]

3.1.2. *The emergence of a common market for structured research*

The promising ISTEX[2] platform has an exceptional mandate. It is a project for centralizing resources since its main objective is to offer, to the entire higher education and research community, online access to retrospective scientific literature collections within all disciplines. It does so by employing a national policy for substantial documentation acquisition"[3].

3.2. The user contributes to the creation and development of content process

3.2.1. *The user in the creative process*

The relationship between the developer and the user is reciprocal. We are faced with a hybridization phase of mutual transformation, where in the end

---

1 Ghislaine Chartron, "Stratégie, Politique et Reformulation de l'Open Access", *Revue Française des Sciences de l'Information et de la Communication.* This translates as "Strategy, Policy and Reformulation of Open Access", which was posted online on 24th March 2016, and we consulted on 29th March 2016, http://rfsic.revues.org/1836.
2 This is the "Excellence Initiative for Scientific and Technical Information".
3 Site of ISTEX: http://www.istex.fr/le-projet/.

new channels of research and innovation are created from extremely disparate sources, which interact in all kinds of ways.

Within the practice of crowdsourcing, the contract issue is particularly live. This is when a business makes an invitation directly for surfers to tender for innovation work online.

Furthermore, the Parisian barristers' chambers the Cabinet Bastien[4] states, "Within the ever-changing open innovation (Chesbrough, 2003), these new methods are interesting to study as they offer a series of new contractual arrangements, organizing the relationship between a purchaser of innovation (the firm) and a seller (the internet user)."

The chambers adds, "The author holds copyright in his work independently of all registration requirements, which implies that the internet user contributor could potentially hold copyright as soon as he contributes to producing creative content sought by the business. (covered by Article L. 111-2 of the Code de la Propriété Intellectuelle[5])."

The Cabinet Bastien goes on, "Furthermore, the process of delivering the production thus demanded through digital media, within the commercial competition framework, should not be interpreted as a transfer of the copyright owned by business internet user. (encompassed in Article L. 111-3 of the Code de la Propriété Intellectuelle)."

The Cabinet Bastien concludes, "It is therefore necessary, within the framework of a crowdsourcing operation, to anticipate operational contracts of original content protected by copyright, to avoid the phenomenon of intellectual parasitism by the company"[6].

3.2.2. *The user in the development process*

Finally, within crowdfunding of scientific projects, equity finance is applied to development. This practice makes it possible to bypass the logic of traditional financing, and makes the user responsible, ensuring that he

---

4 This is run by the barrister Delphine Bastien who specializes in Intellectual Property.
5 This translates to "Intellectual Property Code".
6 http://www.cabinetbastien.fr/publication-19022-les-enjeux-juridiques-du-crowdsourcing.html.

directly contributes to the development process. For example, the Numalire project (which INRA[7] is involved in) is the digitization of ancient books, which is funded through equity finance.

The diagram of the scientific data user is, in reality, multi-dimensional, and may increasingly position itself at various points within the contractual relationship. This contributes to the increasing confusion around intellectual property and the history of science.

In this way, the contract between the developer and the user makes it possible to:

– understand and organize these roles which become increasingly more convergent;

– manage the user's status at each of these particular stages;

– protect the added intellectual and creative value without hindering market efficiency.

---

7 *Institut National de la Recherche Agronomique* (this translates to "the French National Institute for Agricultural Research").

Researchers' Uses and Needs for Scientific and Technical Information

4.1. The CNRS survey

The uses and needs of scientific and technical information (STI) (being the entire bank of information produced through research, which is as necessary to scientific fields as industry) are differentiated by the various research communities. Such uses depend, to some extent, upon so-called "concrete" scientific work, which digital technology overturns.

The *Direction de l'Information Scientifique et Technique* (DIST)[1] of the Centre National de la Recherche Scientifique (CNRS[2]) carried out a survey around STI uses and needs for STI among heads of the CNRS research departments, in mid-2014. The rate of response encompasses approximately one-third of departments (432 respondents). The sample is representative of the 10 CNRS institutes. This survey thus offers STI data with an original soundness and richness from which to draw. Complementary data[3] around

1 This translates as the "Management for Scientific and Technical Information".
2 This translates as the "National Centre for Scientific Research".
3 These data have been gathered on the Internet sites of research departments and through their management, professional networks of the Scientific and Technical Information (STI), the Agence d'Evaluation de la Recherche et de l'Enseignement Supérieur (this is the evaluation agency for research and higher education, known as AERES, which assesses research conducted, staff and qualifications of higher education institutions) and the *Ministry of Higher Education and Research*, and on the academic social network ResearchGate.

collective, scientific and organizational departmental characteristics have been matched with survey data.

This chapter focuses upon three types of descriptive statistics, corresponding to the three questions below:

1) Are STI uses and needs differentiated according to institutes (cross-tabulation)?

2) If yes, are these variables community-dependent (the Pearson χ^2 test)?

3) If yes, depending upon what intensity (using Cramér's V)?

The line of argument in this chapter is based upon using the survey. For clarity of interpretation, only some of the results which proved outstanding are reported. The comprehensive results are available online (see the list of online links at the end of this chapter).

4.1.1. *The 10 CNRS institutes*

Institut des Sciences Biologiques (INSB) – the Institute of Biological Sciences

Institut de Chimie (INC) – the Institute of Chemistry

Institut Ecologie et Environnement (INEE) – the Institute of Ecology and Environment

Institut des Sciences Humaines et Sociales (INSHS) – the Institute of Human and Social Sciences

Institut des Sciences de l'Information et de leurs Interactions (INS2I) – the Institute of Information Sciences and their Interactions

Institut des Sciences de l'Ingéniérie et des Systèmes (INSIS) – the Institute of Engineering Sciences and Systems

Institut National des Sciences Mathématiques (INSMI) – the National Institute of Mathematical Sciences

Institut de Physique (INP) – the Institute of Physics

Institut National de Physique Nucléaire et de Physique des Particules (IN2P3) – the National Institute of Nuclear Physics and Particle Physics

Institut National des Sciences de l'Univers (INSU) – the National Institute of Sciences of the Universe

4.2. Diverse uses and dual needs

In this survey, STI uses are differentiated, to a significant extent, according to scientific communities, and therefore according to the institutes which group them together. This institute-dependency relationship extends over the entire STI production line; that is production, exploitation and development. For example, apparently no research unit attached to the INP includes researchers linked to systematic digitization projects and declared as such. For the INSHS, this rate is around 60% (Table 4.1).

Institute	Yes		No	
	%	Staff numbers	%	Staff numbers
INP	0.00	0	100.00	30
INC	3.70	2	96.30	52
INSB	4.55	3	95.45	63
INSIS	9.76	4	90.24	37
INEE	10.71	3	89.29	25
INS2I	12.90	4	87.10	27
INSMI	21.74	5	78.26	18
INSU	22.58	7	77.42	24
IN2P3	38.46	5	61.54	8
INSHS	59.80	61	40.20	41
Total	22.43	94	77.57	325
Pearson's X^2 test: 123.0996 |Cramér's V (phi): 0.5420				

Table 4.1. *Researchers from the given unit are linked to digitization projects*

Interpretation: "Amongst the heads of units connected to the INP, 0% indicated that researchers from their unit are connected with digitization projects. For the heads of units connected to the INC, the INSB, the INSIS, the INEE, the INS2I, the INSMI, the INSU, the IN2P3 and the INSHS, these proportions are respectively 3.70%, 4.55%, 9.76%, 10.71%, 12.90%, 21.74%, 22.58%, 38.46% and 59.80%. These proportional variations become significant at the threshold level of 0.1%".

Field: All heads of unit. The number of observations is 419.

Source: Survey of the STI needs of the various Institutes (2014) using author calculations

Institute	Yes		No	
	%	Staff numbers	%	Staff numbers
INSHS	63.92	62	36.08	35
INEE	31.03	9	68.97	20
IN2P3	30.77	4	69.23	9
INP	28.57	8	71.43	20
INSIS	27.03	10	72.97	27
INC	25.45	14	74.55	41
INSMI	22.73	5	77.27	17
INSU	22.58	7	77.42	24
INSB	18.46	12	81.54	53
INS2I	16.67	5	83.33	25
Total	33.58	137	66.42	271
Pearson's X^2 test: 58.1441 |Cramér's V (phi): 0.3775				

Table 4.2. *Support requirements for the unit's provision through digital services used for publishing assistance*

Interpretation: "Amongst the heads of unit attached to the INSHS, 63.92% require the department's publishing provision to be supported by digital services for publishing assistance. For the heads of research units connected to the INEE, the IN2P3, the INP, the INSIS, the INC, the INSMI, the INSU, the INSB and the INS2I, these proportions are respectively 31.03%, 30.77%, 28.57%, 27.03%, 25.45%, 22.73%, 22.58%, 18.46% and 16.67%. These proportional variations become significant at the threshold level of 0.1% ".

Field: All heads of unit. The number of observations is 408.

Source: Survey of the STI needs of the various Institutes (2014) using author calculations

However, STI requirements display a remarkable duality. Generally, in contrast, there are a primary group of user institutes, which support the application of STI for digital publishing (mainly INSHS, followed by the INEE). There is also a second group which proves to be more reluctant to use such an application. For example, there are approximately 64% of research units attached to the INSHS that require their unit's publishing provision to be supported by digital services in publishing assistance. This rate reduces to 31% for the INEE and 23% for the INSMI (Table 4.2).

4.3. An explanation through differentiated scientific analysis

How can we explain this paradox? The survey makes it possible to summarize three explanations.

For the institutes appealing for support, STI is an entirely separate task. Simultaneously within institutes that have low support demand, STI might constitute the substance of researchers' work. For the first group of institutes, STI demands skills (dedicated staff) and specific planning (for example financing and management plans), while within the second group, it is the responsibility of the researchers themselves. Within the first group, STI necessitates a significant data management task (this includes the functions of reformatting and meta-description), which occurs to a lesser extent within the second group.

It is indeed a collective concern (involving, for example, practices for co-construction and collaboration) in the first group, and is more distinctive in the second case. Thus, for example, approximately 81, 59 and 55% of the INSU, the INS2I and the INSHS units respectively make their databases available online. This compares to approximately 8% of the INSMI of departments (Table 4.3).

Institute	Yes		No	
	%	Staff numbers	%	Staff numbers
INSU	81.25	26	18.75	6
INS2I	59.09	13	40.91	9
INSHS	55.32	52	44.68	42
INEE	51.85	14	48.15	13
IN2P3	50.00	6	50.00	6
INSB	43.55	27	56.45	35
INSIS	33.33	12	66.67	24
INC	29.41	15	70.59	36
INP	24.00	6	76.00	19
INSMI	7.69	1	92.31	12
Total	45.87	172	54.13	203
Pearson's X^2 test: 42.8050	Cramér's V (phi): 0.3379				

Table 4.3. *The department databases are accessible online*

The institutes that require STI are handling particularly sensitive data, whether, as examples, personal data (the INSHS) or patented data (the INEE). They are faced to a larger extent by legal questions (for example digitization, posting online, reuse and making data content available, data development and open data). For example, respectively, approximately 64 and 62% of unit heads of the INSHS and the INEE have already been faced with legal questions concerning digitization and posting content online (Table 4.4).

The institutes which are unwilling to use STI support have already tightly structured their STI use. Their departments share universal standards (such as publication rules). They use the interdisciplinary open data archive known as HAL in abundance[4], as well as disciplinary open data archives (for example the INSMI uses DBLP[5]), specialized in IT. The INSMI is distinguished by STI professional networks, which are particularly dynamic

4 Hyper Articles en Ligne (HAL).
5 Digital Bibliography & Library Project.

communities, such as the Réseau National des Bibliothèques de Mathématiques (RNBM))[6].

Institute	Yes		No	
	%	Staff numbers	%	Staff numbers
INSHS	63.54	61	36.46	35
INEE	61.54	16	38.46	10
IN2P3	54.55	6	45.45	5
INS2I	46.67	14	53.33	16
INSU	29.03	9	70.97	22
INSB	23.08	15	76.92	50
INC	20.75	11	79.25	42
INSIS	18.92	7	81.08	30
INP	14.29	4	85.71	24
INSMI	10.53	2	89.47	17
Total	36.78	146	63.22	251
Pearson's X^2 test: 69.6036 |Cramér's V (phi): 0.4187				

Table 4.4. *Extent to which institutes have been previously faced with legal questions concerning digitization and placing department content online*

Beyond uses which are unique to each institute, characteristics which are common to scientific work (for example scientific status, legal features and STI community structuring) give rise to two types of STI needs. These are either a greater or lesser demand for support. In the former case, in particular, the INSHS and the INEE feature to a lesser extent. In the second case, the INSMI, in particular, features. This duality of needs appreciates the opportunities for STI service offers, which are interoperable for these two groups of institutes.

Interpretation: "Out of all of the heads of departments linked with the INSU, 81.25% have databases which are accessible online. For heads of unit attached to the INS2I, the INSHS, the INEE, the IN2P3, the INSB, the INSIS, the INC, the INP and the INSMI, these proportions are respectively

---

6 This translates as "the National Network of Mathematical Libraries".

59.09%, 55.32%, 51.85%, 50.00%, 43.55%, 33.33%, 29.41%, 24.00% and 7.69%. These proportional variations become significant at the threshold level of 0.1%".

Field: All heads of unit. The number of observations is 375.

Source: Survey of the STI needs of the various Institutes (2014) using author calculations

Interpretation: "Out of heads of units attached to INSHS, 63.54% state that they have previously been faced with legal issues concerning digitization and posting content held by their department online. For heads of units linked to the INEE, the IN2P3, the INS2I, the INSU, the INSB, the INC, the INSIS, the INP and the INSMI, these proportions are respectively 61.54%, 54.55%, 46.67%, 29.03%, 23.08%, 20.75%, 18.92%, 14.29% and 10.53%. These proportional variations become significant at the threshold level of 0.1%."

Field: All heads of unit. The number of observations is 397.

Source: Survey of the STI needs of the various Institutes (2014) using author calculations

New Tools for Knowledge Capture

"I dreamed of a world (in which computers) became capable of analyzing all data on the World Wide Web – content, links, and transactions between individuals and computers. *A "Semantic Web", which ought to make this possible, has not yet emerged, but when this happens, the day-to-day exchange mechanisms, the bureaucracy and our daily lives will all be managed by machines interacting with other machines. So-called 'intelligent agents' which we have promised ourselves for a long time will finally materialize*"[1] (Tim Berners-Lee).

5.1. The growth of metadata exploitation

5.1.1. *The growth of the use of metadata*

5.1.1.1. *Through social networks…*

The use of metadata is booming. This is first happening through targeting. For example, Facebook is launching its search engine, indexing all of its public content. By knowing the interests of each user, this search engine will be able to suggest highly targeted responses and organize results tailored to individual needs.

In the same spirit, Google has entered the social networks sector using Google+. This allows it to collect new data and thus to better target research results.

---

1 Tim Berners-Lee, Mark Fischetti, *Weaving the Web*, Harper, San Francisco, 1999.

5.1.1.2. ...and by way of knowledge creation

The example of Watson is a good illustration of how metadata exploitation could herald a revolution. It is a supercomputer, designed by IBM[2], which is contributing to the fight against lung cancer. Fed permanently by a multitude of data (whether articles, medical results and other data), it possesses the capacity to, at once, integrate it, analyze it and establish connections between such data. This makes it possible to put forward hypotheses, to justify and verify them. We might thus reach conclusions that traditional research means would have attained, although in a far longer time. Indeed, its capacity for analysis (even in terms of data quantity) far surpasses that of any human being.

Furthermore, doctors can submit a patient's case to the computer and send him the analysis results. The computer thus suggests possible diagnoses both according to likelihood and appropriate treatment.

The use of metadata is therefore a key to artificial intelligence, since it gives the machine the capacity to analyze data, and to adapt, paving the way for genuine knowledge creation.

5.2. Are we moving toward a semantic Web?

5.2.1. Definition

With the Web constantly evolving, there are various hypotheses around what could be the next major revolution, that is Web 3.0. One of the most considerable (with the advent of the hypothesis of an Internet of Things) is the emergence of a semantic web[3].

The latter, which is also known as "Linked Data", is defined by Tim Berners-Lee, as "a data Web which may be processed directly and indirectly by machines to aid users in creating new knowledge." Lee also theorizes about the Giant Global Graph (GGG), which is a form of semantic Web with a higher level of decentralization.

---

2 http://www-05.ibm.com/fr/watson/.
3 http://www.enssib.fr/le-dictionnaire/web-semantique.

5.2.2. *Web evolution [MUR 11]*

Web 1.0 is a passive form of Web Data circulating vertically, from one user who creates content to another who consumes it.

Web 2.0 is collaborative.It makes collective involvement in the creation of information possible. The classic example is Wikipedia: everyone can be a reader and a player, with the opportunity for data enrichment. It is therefore the sum of the knowledge of a group of people.

Although Tim Berners-Lee's intuition has been confirmed, Web 3.0 (or the semantic Web) might make possible data linking, not only of data but also of metadata. Accessible knowledge may not be therefore limited to that which users directly write, but also includes machine-extracted knowledge from the crossroads between such data.

Figure 5.1. *From Web 1.0. to Web 3.0*

5.3. Tools and limits for metadata processing

5.3.1. *Tools being developed*

The two main objectives in data processing are the following: extracting metadata and classifying it into categories. Although some tools are starting to appear, the potential for improvement remains large.

5.3.2. *Capturing metadata*

It is quite simple for an organization to use metadata which is "given up" by users (whether consciously or not): their connection time, the time a message is sent, the identity of users contacted by that organization and its geo-tracking. The stakes, so as to go further in capturing metadata, nowadays involve processing the content of the metadata itself.

Indeed, although the metadata may be directly readable (and therefore able to be processed) by a machine, the majority of the data are not. The computer will thus be able to identify a file such as a photo, knowing its size, weight and format. However, it will not know what it shows.

As a means of capturing and extracting metadata, we may mention the bibliographical management software Mendeley. This software makes it possible to copy PDF documents and their metadata and to link all such information according to such data. This thus makes efficient research possible. The software eSniff plays a similar role within the scientific sphere.

5.3.3. *Classification of metadata*

In relation to the classification of data, numerous concepts emerge, for example ontology, text mining, semantic mapping and folksonomy. All of these are aiming to categorize data, text or metadata and create links between it. The aim is, having captured a very large quantity of data, to link it together to draw meaning from this, to elicit conclusions and in a word to create knowledge.

5.4. The challenges of the semantic Web

There are major challenges in the creation of Web 3.0. Tim Berners-Lee thus started to speak of a semantic Web in 2001, and although the idea is progressing little-by-little, the means have not yet materialized.

5.4.1. *The main technical difficulties*

First, the number of documents and data is vast. Consequently, the project site is on a very large scale. Another difficulty lies in encoding the text itself. The principal coding language for Web documents is HTML. Yet, this language makes no link between the document texts, which brings into question the possibility of a semantic Web. It does not know how to detect the nature of particular signs in a document (for example that a particular word is a price, and another an object, or even that they are linked). It simply considers them as pieces of text which must be placed next to each other.

However, other languages are able to make these links (and therefore a semantic Web) possible, for example RDF, OWL and WML. However, these are not the most frequently used. It would need many more documents to be coded in these languages, so that links can be established between all of these data, and thus allow for it to be processed separately.

5.4.2. *Data ranking*

Finally, the issue of data ranking crops up. Data posted by users are inaccurate, often uncertain and unestablished. All sources do not therefore carry the same worth. Data should not only be captured but also ranked, so as to be efficiently processed by a semantic Web.

The real innovation offered by the semantic Web therefore rests in the fact that the tools can become players which themselves are entirely separate from knowledge creation. This is achieved by linking data between them which is, in fact, artificial intelligence. However that assumes capturing data, which may be processed through using a machine and ranking the data. Encoding tools and appropriate analysis should therefore be implemented.

6

Modes of Knowledge
Sharing and Technologies

Scientific research, far from being the source of a series of fixed dogmas, is constantly evolving, as it is a debate between several hypotheses. These hypotheses may or may not then be confirmed by experiments. This debate is made possible by knowledge sharing between both members of the scientific community and between the scientific community and the public. Knowledge sharing, which is thus so vital for scientific research, is nowadays accelerated by the use of modern technologies.

6.1. Data storage technologies and access allowing knowledge sharing

The acceleration of knowledge sharing nowadays happens through digitally linked technologies at the knowledge storage level, and through everyone's access to these.

6.1.1. *Databases*

Storage happens across the databases, which are structured data sets. Both of the databases "Pascal" and "Francis", owned by l'INIST (Institut de l'Information Scientifique et Technique[1]), the institute attached to the

---

1 This translates to the "Institute of Scientific and Technical Data".

CNRS, each have a specific role. "Pascal" is responsible for storing knowledge linked to human and social sciences (HSS), while the "Francis" database is the equivalent for knowledge sharing in the sphere of sciences, technologies and medicine (STM).

Due to these databases, nearly 20 million biographical references (the earliest of which dates back to 1973) are stored. The preservation of these databases thus greatly facilitates the sharing of scientific informational archives between researchers.

These databases are still being enriched nowadays, due to partnerships such as that concluded in 2013 between Abes (Agence Bibliographique de l'Enseignement Supérieur[2]) and l'INIST, which increases the number of thesis documents held on "Francis" each year by 1,500[3].

6.2. Exchange platforms and catalogs

Knowledge sharing also takes place through exchange platforms such as CorIST, where members of the scientific community are able to discuss their research results.

So that knowledge sharing is not limited to the scientific community and that controversial debate is broadened to the public, various tools should allow for open access to this knowledge. This means of knowledge transmission, above all, takes the form of online catalogs such as Refdoc or OPAC, on the CNRS Internet site.

They indeed cover literature within HSS and STM from a period from 1901 to the end of 2014, with a total of 115,000 reports of French and international scientific conferences. Other tools such as thematic knowledge portals are also used[4].

Finally, digital libraries such as the ISTEX project[5] make access to each of these forms of knowledge possible.

---

2 This translates as "the Higher Education Bibliographical Agency".
3 http://www.inist.fr/?FRANCIS.
4 http://www.inist.fr/?-Portails-&lang=fr.
5 http://www.inist.fr/?Istex&lang=fr.

6.3. Knowledge-processing and digital editions

To facilitate knowledge sharing and, to this end, accelerate scientific research, document-processing tools are made available to researchers. One of these tools is the DOI or the Digital Object Identifier which makes it possible to identify, in a unique way, each physical and digital object stemming from research and to send the researcher to reliable online resources[6]. The registration center of DOI, which is able to operate similarly to a search engine, is called DataCite. The organization INIST-CNRS is a member of this. Another example of this type of tool is the French-German project Quaero, the objective of which is to facilitate the processing of multimedia content.

Digital publications also make this knowledge-sharing possible, with examples such as *I-Revues*[7], which publishes scientific reviews, symposiums and electronic books or LARA[8], which publishes technical and scientific reports. A recent example of knowledge sharing is MOOCs or Massive Open Online Courses. These are free Internet access-based courses, and therefore accessible to the greatest number of individuals[9].

Within the structuring between the sciences, in the sense of knowledge, technologies and uses, knowledge sharing by digital technologies and through their use, which increases daily, is thus at the center of scientific research.

---

6 http://www.inist.fr/?Attribution-de-DOI&lang=fr.
7 http://irevues.inist.fr.
8 http://lara.inist.fr.
9 https://www.youtube.com/watch?v=_o5WW64r1DE.

PART 2

Sharing Mechanisms:
Knowledge Sharing and the
Knowledge-based Economy

7

Business Model for Scientific Publication

Access to scientific publications, technologies and past research is facilitated by the multiplicity of supports and increasing linkages which exist between the various research centers. It increasingly poses problems around profitability, modifying the economic model of scientific publication.

Whether it is a question of "author" financing or a dual "reader-author" financing, "a global explanation is being put together" according to a CNRS report from June 2015 entitled "Financing scientific publication"[1].

This is a genuine digital halo, bringing together both unpublished and unfinished material, which undermines knowledge sharing, knowledge use and, eventually, scientific evolution.

7.1. The current economic model is changing so as to adapt to new conditions for knowledge sharing

7.1.1. *A former model currently under discussion*

7.1.1.1. *A scientific publication which is widely subject to private publishers*

As far back as 1665, the first exclusively scientific review of history was published, known as the Philosophical Transactions of the Royal Society. It

1 This is available at: http://www.cnrs.fr/dist/z-outils/documents/Distinfo2/DISTetude_4.pdf.

set in motion a long-term movement within the publishing world, which has since progressively developed an entire sector specializing in scientific publishing.

Today, international scientific publishing is a genuine field of conflicts and forces, where the stances of the various players are vigorously guarded. In 2014, there were 12 major international publishers sharing a market of around 12.8 billion dollars, in particular major U.S. publishing houses which are internationally recognized. The most significant include Springer, Reed Elsevier, Taylor & Francis and Wiley.

Private publishers operate using the *"Big Deal" principle*, which rests upon contracts for license usage: this provide their users with access to all resources owned by the publisher. Such a system provides unquestionable added user value, ensuring both data formatting and bibliographical clarification. Smaller publishers have difficulty aligning themselves with the market when faced with the scale of the catalog of the largest publishing houses.

The very large international so-called "independent" publishers have at their disposal significant capacity-building strategies and innovation potential. These rest upon great investment power. They also have the know-how ensuring that they have a position which is difficult to contest within the market. This involves marketing, commercial services and support functions.

In these circumstances, the initiatives of the public and university sectors to open up the sharing of scientific knowledge suffer during downturns.

Traditionally, two types of financing are adopted for scientific reviews. First, there is financing through "subscriptions" taken out in libraries – that is, the readers – to be able to both access content and exploit it.

This finance model is unquestionably becoming less and less effective, given the accessibility of Internet content and unauthorized sharing of some scientific research which enables forgery.

Meanwhile, an author-based financing model is developing. It operates through the use of Article Processing Charges (APCs). These are publication costs paid by authors themselves to see their work published in a scientific publication.

7.1.2. *A model changed drastically by the presence of NICTs*

While NICTs make it possible to maintain a permanent link between different authors, the traditional model to finance scientific publications no longer seems to respond adequately to market demand. Scientists often prefer publications which use new free media platforms, which are available on the Internet or by open sharing. They publish their research upon such platforms, producing better results than using a dedicated review.

In this way, regarding the increased growth of knowledge, scientists and researchers alike agree that both methods making up the former model no longer operate properly. It is necessary to find a new plan for wealth distribution and production within the scientific community. In its report mentioned above, the CNRS concludes by explaining that "the system for financing publication is currently in midstream".

7.2. Creation of a new model

7.2.1. *Toward a so-called "open process"?*

The European Union's External Relations Committee and numerous other players were recently revealed as organizing a new form of financing for scientific publishing. Among the alternatives suggested, the implementation of an open process by replacing the APC of the financing model by the authors increasingly appeals to scientific committees.

Ensuring low-cost publications would be a matter of developing new conditions for the "peer review" of scientific content by making use of automated digital tools.

This is the case with text mining – such as text search support. However, this is also more broadly the opportunity to widen and modernize the concepts of intellectual property within scientific publishing, through the new regime of intellectual property for Creative Commons, which offers a managed form of content release. Henceforth, researchers will be paid by researching-funding organizations or universities wishing to increase their prestige with the success of their lecturers.

7.2.2. *Moving toward open access*

The aim of this new model is also to facilitate reader access by open access, that is to say the availability of online publications, whether they are indeed protected by the traditional legal system or fall outside of the legal regime. The means and publication support media are thus increased, simplified, automated and brought into widespread use. This may notably happen via the deployment of the national digital archive HAL in France for the CNRS.

Open access offers a dual revolution. This occurs by sharing knowledge in the public domain by bringing into widespread use access to research works, by offering scientists more significant means of communication.

For these virtues, the new model for open access attracts a large number of capital investors who wish to participate in the development of publication frameworks. There are therefore multiple issues, and all of the problems linked to the emergence of a new economic model are thus not yet resolved.

7.3. The issues raised by the creation of a new economic model

7.3.1. *Appearance of a digital halo*

Scientific and technical information benefits from the advantage of a wide audience and a better dissemination through the Internet. However, a "digital halo" seems to be taking shape, with the emergence of a scientific publication which is formed as vague and disorganized. Three elements combine to make up this halo:

1) the emergence of a lost science. This is an issue relating to all digital scientific publications which do not wish to follow the classic online model

and assume discreet and unknown dissemination channels, or all scientific data finalized for presentation (thus, for example, in articles) but not reserved for publication and therefore risk being lost. This brings up one of the major problems of scientific publication. Each piece of research or article is, in general, classified according to its citations; the absence of this lost science in classification methods creates a dangerous vacuum. Moreover, quality publications may no longer be profitable. The UN and the International Council for Science are both currently speaking in favor of the homogenization of international publication standards;

2) the loss of IST, or unused data which accumulate over time. There is a genuine difference between the amount of scientific and technical data produced and the number of publications which are produced. According to an Elsevier study conducted in 2014[2], 90% of data produced may remain unused. It is considered that this significant amount of unused data is a real danger for the publication itself. The more both platforms and methods increase, the more legal data capture disappears in favor of illegal appropriation. Among the most significant issues of the new economic model of scientific publication, "listing and publishing data" in order to facilitate its publication across the various platforms which develop seems to play an essential role;

3) a willingness for transparency. Numerous initiatives appear to encourage the bringing together of information. The site Retraction Watch[3] publishes so-called "ill-conducted" scientific experiments. It states all publications which have been withdrawn on account of being judged fraudulent, in particular through peer review software. Plagiarism is avoided owing to tools such as Crosscheck, which are set up by numerous publishers to give authors the entitlements due to them. It is also a matter of controlling malevolent publishers, who offer no financial contribution to the level of their use of scientific data. A list of malevolent open access publishers was established and is updated frequently by Jeffrey Beall, a librarian specializing in witch-hunting scientific publications.

---

2 Elsevier's Disruptive Technologies Department. See the detailed results of the study in the DIST report and the publication Scientifique Aujourd'hui (Science Today).
3 www.retractionwatch.com.

7.4. A new economic model struggling to find its niche

The new economic model desired by readers and scientific players suffers even more on account of its early development phase.

For the past seven years, the annual Open Access Week has been held to promote this. The 2015 event proved the occasion upon which to recall that open access is, from now on, a truly integral part of the publication landscape. David Crotty, who specializes in the issue, claims that "We cannot deny the increase and growing acceptance of Open Access in the scientific publication world. However, the repercussions for the economic model and Open Access methods selected have barely been acknowledged".

He states in his blog that the problems pertaining to the new economic model are not ready to be settled. Firstly, because the largest publishers continue to reap the major part of publication income. Significant income stemming from open access, due to the concentration of power and the economies of scale, is made possible by the size of their structures. Secondly, because libraries work to assume administrative expenses due to bad financial management linked to the immaturity of open access depositaries. Finally, because the costs of the open access depositaries within the former publication structures are becoming less and less pertinent given the emergence of more lucrative networks such as Research Gate and Academia.edu, criticized for their mercantile logic.

Thus, it clearly appears that the modernization of methods of publication, communication and research tools has favored the emergence of numerous platforms. They have lowered the barriers to entry for scientists, who wish to make their research known to the world.

However, this increase in excess support media has led to the emergence of a "digital halo" with perverse effects. Centralization has been made impossible and scientific nebulae have emerged. The current question for the health of the economic model for scientific publications, and therefore evidently for the continuity of scientific research, is how to create a model possessing new established boundaries, without leaving any scope for fraud, and which gives free reign to the field of ideas. The UN is encouraging this.

Actor Strategy: International Scientific Publishing, Services with High Added Value and Research Communities

The establishment of an international scientific publishing industry has boosted the supply of articles. Faced with the increase in reviews and articles, often neglecting quality in favor of quantity, a social scientist such as Arnaud de Saint-Martin envisages a form of "junk science"[1]. This is a science which happens quickly and lacks substance. It is entirely a question of *how* to spread – and therefore create – science which is at stake here. The latter is not happening at a regular pace, and is therefore subject to ever harsher publication constraints in such a way that open access starts to redefine itself.

This argument may be found in two affairs, one fairly recent – the Maffesoli affair[2] – and the other dating back to the 1990s. The first shows how an article containing false information was able to be published in a sociology review, to the detriment of truly introspective interpretation. There is a deeper echo to the second affair, the Sokal affair (or the Sokal hoax)[3], in which Alain Sokal, a doctor, had published a fake document in the

---

1 http://www.lemonde.fr/education/article/2015/03/10/la-revue-societes-piegee-par-deux-sociologues_4590914_1473685.html.

2 http://sciences.blogs.liberation.fr/home/2015/03/un-canular-sociologique-d%C3%A9cortique-le-maffesolisme.html.

3 https://lhomme.revues.org/86.

publication *Social Text*, so as to denounce the explosion of the postmodern language. These two examples show a single point; the crystallization of tensions around scientific publishing, through its excesses, in particular, with false information.

We should understand that for a researcher, publishing is a way of life. We should use the vectors of the scientific institution, or the publishers. Within the entirety of this field of publication, it is therefore quite easy to understand the underlying issues. Indeed, by simplifying the issues we encounter two strategies; one of recognition (on the part of researchers) and one of an economic strategy (on the part of publishers). How should we analyze the junction between the two? Are they antithetical? Can we say that international scientific publishing constitutes science in its true form? Alternatively, are research communities, through open access and a policy of publishing in the public domain, needed to buck the trend?

8.1. Publishing, editing and existing: live issues within the publication of Scientific and Technical Information (STI)

8.1.1. *Publishers' sources of power*

Pierre Bourdieu says, "the publisher is one with a quite extraordinary power to ensure publication, that is to say to make both a known and recognized text and author accessible to the public domain"[4]. This publishing power may also be explained by the influence of the various international publishing houses. This is vast, concentrated upon highly precise segments, and relatively oligopolistic. What structure does international scientific publishing take?

Large publishers developed by progressively purchasing small reviews, then by purchasing the journals which, at that time, lacked the funds to make the transition to digital, thus enlarging U.S. publishing houses. A large training movement for editorial or thematic packaging was then set in motion. Nowadays, there are no less than 30,000 review titles, being a mix

---

4 http://www.persee.fr/doc/arss_0335-5322_1999_num_126_1_3278.

of STM and SMS. For examples of these large publishing houses, we may mention *Elsevier*[5], *Springer*[6], *Taylor & Francis*[7] and *Wiley*[8].

These journals themselves are businesses, launched to make money and not specifically for scientific breakthroughs. Their economic model thus ties up with blatant profitability, which is opposed to the stages of social science profitability.

8.2. Who is subject to it? The other players in scientific publishing

For research institutions and researchers, subscription and publication costs have become excessively high, literally exceeding hundreds of thousands of euros for the most notorious publications (for example JStor[9]). In particular, there are some predatory publishers which take advantage of the appeal offered by open access with author payment, and consequently complicate the potential for researchers to publish their works. This environment enhances a form of social competition, which is diluted between the various players and their respective strategies.

Despite these economic constraints, reviews and large international scientific publishers wield power over researchers due to their impact factor. The latter is an ulterior motive on their part, which demonstrates the position of a given review. This visibility is sought by researchers, who are more or less certain of widening their readership as a result of an increased impact factor. This impact also determines the rankings (1st, 2nd, 3rd, etc.) which define the international recognition of a journal. The scientific journals *Nature* or *Science* are thus the two most highly-rated journals. With their elevated impact factors, such publications ensure clear visibility for every researcher publishing therein.

The dependency of researchers on scientific publishing is strong and contributes less and less to science. As Dominique Cardon explains: "A

---

5 http://www.elsevier.com.

6 http://www.springer.com.

7 http://taylorandfrancis.com/.

8 http://eu.wiley.com/WileyCDA/.

9 http://www.jstor.org/.

performance indicator, which is often unique, becomes an interpretation tool in a far more general context. The reflexiveness of meters has increasingly made players strategists."[10] We are witnessing the confusion of roles and objectives, with publication profits which are becoming excessive.

Peer-reviewing represents research capture in publishing houses. The prestige of a given journal also happens according to the presence of a distinguished peer review committee. Scientific recognition may also be calculated (the H-index is the best example of this). It is on the basis of these bibliometric indices that careers may develop or rewards be reaped. Publication is an actual and concrete visibility, which does not appear possible for the researcher themself to bring about.

What is more, access becomes compulsory through the structure of the economic system. The costs of access are exorbitant, as has been shown by the recent price increase at Elsevier. The net margin is close to 35% for publishers, according to a very recent CNRS report[11]. Faced with this dependency, negotiations are then arranged. This is the case with the Couperin consortium[12] in France, which brings together universities and research centers so as to decrease the overall subscription cost. Despite these negotiations, the economics of international scientific publishing remains highly competitive, especially at research level, the level of which has now increased for several years. This is increasingly the case in emerging countries such as China, where the University of Science and Technology is one of the institutions which generates the most published works in the world.

8.3. The characteristics of SMS (Science of Man and Society)

The entire international publishing sphere and its recognition differs according to both the national field and the scientific field. Let us take the example of the SMS.

---

10 Dominique Cardon, "A quoi rêvent les algorithmes. Nos vies à l'heure des big data", *La République des idées*, 2015 [This translates as "How algorithms dream. Our lives in the big data era"].

11 http://www.cnrs.fr/dist/z-outils/documents/Distinfo2/DISTetude3.pdf.

12 http://www.couperin.org/.

8.3.1. *The national character of SMSs*

SMSs possess a far more centralized national nature than wider physical or medical applications. The international journals being written in English, there are choices to make and these are regularly theoretical articles which either are translated into or initially written in English. It is the same thing with an epistemological or thematic focus. May we thus export the highly geographically specific ethnographic fields and publish them within high-ranking journals? This is, for example, the case when French publications are exported into the *American Sociological Review*[13], where theoretical and general articles, which are easily transferable from one sphere to another, are predominantly published. This concern opposes the specialization which exists within social science publishing, where the number of journals continues to increase, with specializations per given institutions or by themes. The GFII report *"L'Édition Scientifique Française en Sciences Sociales et Humaines"*[14] from 2009 stated that only 2% of the 540 important and major journals are found within international publishers' catalogs.

8.3.2. *The specific temporality and profitability of SMSs*

The second characteristic trait of SMSs is their temporality. The proven scientific character of a given SMS article is established over 10, 60 or even 100 years. Can the same model be applied to both SMSs and STMs, for which 6 months are enough to invalidate a theory?

Finally, if the economic increase in value largely predominates the scientific publication of STMs, it is more complicated to provide a net evaluation for SMSs. Do innovations in human and social sciences, which are applicable to the economic world, actually exist? May we convert sociological, historical and anthropological theories into tradable products, or economic goods to which we may award a given price?

It thus appears that international scientific publishing crystallizes economic and institutional problems. On the one hand, the publishing world increases the value of publication returns, by imposing exorbitant tariffs for

---

13 http://asr.sagepub.com/.
14 This translates as "French Scientist Publication in the Social and Human Sciences". http://www.gfii.fr/fr/document/l-edition-scientifique-francaise-en-sciences-sociales-et-humaines.

research centers and universities. However, it is these same journals which make or break both a researcher's reputation and social position. Is it consequently possible to exist in this sphere without actually publishing?

8.4. Existing without publishing? New STI directions

8.4.1. *New STI tools*

STI has found new tools on the part of international scientific publishers, which have sought to modernize so as to assert their monopoly. They have renewed their service offering by developing high added value services, making it possible to prove their worth in the scientific field.

As Yves Gingras explains, "The field of journals has become a highly competitive market and increasingly uses its 'impact factor' as a promotional tool"[15].

Services with high added value in international scientific publishing are an activity which involves primary source document enrichment. They become indispensable through the knowledge of the scientific network which they possess. It is the centralization of supply which has led to the appearance of high added value services for major publishing houses. In this sense, we find two major service types:

---

15 Yves Gingras, *Les dérives de l'évaluation de la recherche. Du bon usage de la bibliométrie*, Raisons d'agir, 2014 – this translates as "The Excesses of Research Evaluation. Proper Use of Bibliometrics".

– consultation services;

– research services.

For example, publishers have developed monitoring tools, cross-referencing review, magazines, indexing features or enhanced navigability. Elsevier has developed for several years the search engine *Scopus*[16], which cross-references and facilitates research. On a global level, almost collectively, we encounter the software *Crossref*[17].

These services are permanently being reconfigured. We are, for example, witnessing an application of policies of compulsory depositing in open archives as a basic trend. Although it is likely that these open archives are not threatening review subscription revenue, they may have a negative impact on secondary receipts, which rightly link to the exploitation and development of archives of publishing collections. International scientific publishers thus ensure a service monopoly, as well as gains linked to their specificity and the originality of their services. Indeed, these high value added services are substantial investments, which free portals may initiate with difficulty, such as *Cairn*[18] or *Persée*[19] within French SMSs. Entry costs block competition for this high added value and offer a form of renewal of the oligopoly for major publishers.

8.5. Alternatives to scientific publishing

Although these high added value services characterize new strategies for international publishing, we should also stress that research communities offer an alternative path for the issue of scientific publication. Does open science or participatory science signal the end of publishing the single publication?

These solutions are still marginal when faced with scientific constraints which endure for significant periods. A long-established French initiative, that of CNRS and HAL[20] (Hyper-Articles onLine, a commonly used open

16 http://www.scopus.com/.
17 http://www.crossref.org/.
18 http://www.cairn.info/.
19 http://www.persee.fr/.
20 https://hal.archives-ouvertes.fr/.

archive) created in 2001, is worth mentioning in this context. However, this centralized example shows that on a broader level, the lack of coordination between researchers and the pooling difficulty remain recurring barriers. European science and open access policy, nevertheless, offer logical institutional backing for this type of initiative. CNRS thus remains a major player in this development, with an increasing opening for these data. At a later stage, social networks for researchers appeared to unite reflections surrounding the post-scientific publishing phase. This is a societal issue for the scientific world, since the bibliometrics and recognition indices would be entirely transformed.

The institutional power of some research units and institutions such as the CNRS or Ministère de l'Enseignement Supérieur et de la Recherche[21] seems to be one of the strengths upon which the development of open science should rely. Consequently, how should a policy of publishing in the public domain be defined? It seems, taking into account the rigidities and economic oligopolies of international publishers, that a "soft transition" is necessary, to paraphrase the CNRS.

It is therefore as much a reconciliation of strategies, an economic and institutional coordination, as well as a policy of publishing in the public domain, which seems able to maintain the idea of having another structure for international scientific publishing.

Figure 8.1. *HAL (Hyper Articles en Ligne) open archive; CNRS, dépasser les frontières ("push the boundaries")*

---

21 This translates to "Ministry of Higher Education and Research".

However, does openness genuinely provide access? Is it perhaps not the case that the power of high added value services proposed by publishers is too large for public or research institutions to bear the costs of research and consultation?

9

New Approaches to Scientific Production

As researchers are not paid for the pure production of knowledge, the issues around the publication of results are a top priority, owing to the functions that publication provides.

Resuming a typology established by Michael Mabe[1], we may thus distinguish the various roles assumed by the publication process. These are registration, certification, sharing and archiving.

9.1. New means of access to scientific production: innovative models

Although scientific production has not fundamentally changed in nature, its means of access is dramatically changing.

9.1.1. *In favor of optimizing publication and scientific collaboration*

Above and beyond the current thinking, advocating open access to scientific production, and in particular the open access which we have already evoked, we are witnessing the emergence of innovative forms of publication, based upon an innovative certification model.

---

1 M.A. Mabe, "Scholarly publishing", European Review, 2009, mentioned in a paper by C. Berthaud C., L. Capelli *et al.*, "Episciences – an overlay publication platform", IOS Press, 2014.

These forms are devoted, as their main objectives, to both a greater transparency and a better quality of review, greater control of publication by the scientific community, and finally optimizing knowledge sharing and collaboration between researchers.

9.1.1.1. *A new review paradigm toward greater transparency and reliability: episcience*

The classic paradigm for scientific publishing rests upon a post-evaluation publication system by one's peer group. When a researcher submits an article to a scientific review, the publisher must decide whether the article is, *a priori*, authentic, and, if need be, send it for authentication and comments prior to publication. Open archives or reservoirs such as arXiv[2] and HAL[3] have for a long time been devoted to the principle of "pre-prints". Articles may be filed and consulted before they are subject to peer review.

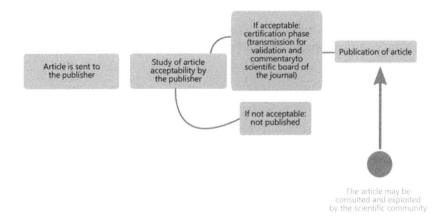

Figure 9.1. *Traditional post-evaluation publication model*

Since this publication model has been taken up by scientific journals, as with the biology and medicine journal PeerJ[4], completed in 2013 by the so-called Peer serviceJ PrePrints, this allows researchers to post online

2 https://arxiv.org/.
3 https://hal.archives-ouvertes.fr.
4 https://peerj.com/.

versions of articles which have not been reviewed, but also drafts or incomplete versions of articles.

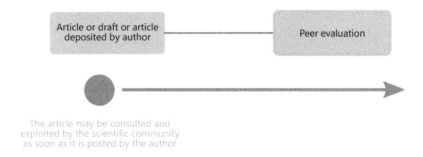

Figure 9.2. *Pre-review (pre-print) publication model*

Several scientists have worked on the basis of the open archives such as HAL or arXiv, and started from the observation that 80% of publishers' work is completed by the actual researchers on an unpaid basis (writing, formatting as well as correction and review of articles). They have partnered up with other scientists to create the platform Episciences in 2013[5], boosted by the CCSD[6] (the Centre Communication Scientifique Directe[7]) in France.

The idea at the heart of the Episciences project is to rethink the process of certification which is ordinarily organized by scientific publishers. Selecting prepublications which already exist on open archives, specialist researchers gather into an editorial board which adds to these articles a level of certification, by reviewing them and discussing them. Articles thus reviewed by editorial boards are brought together as overlay journals, which are available on open access.

By organizing the certification process directly between experts in this way, even within the scientific community, overlay journals open an alternative path to the traditional publishing model by allowing article publication for a minimum cost. Since the Episciences project began, other

---

5 http://www.episciences.org/.
6 This translates to the "Open Scientific Communication Center".
7 https://www.ccsd.cnrs.fr.

scientific teams have undertaken the management of overlay journals, such as the *Discrete Analysis*[8] journals of mathematician Timothy Gowers. For this, the cost of article submission does not exceed $10[9]. All are pursuing a model of so-called diamond open access (which works on the basis of free to read, free to publish) and thus enables the recapturing of scientific publishing by the research community.

Figure 9.3. *Overlay journal model: an alternative to the traditional model*

9.1.2. *Moving toward open peer review with greater transparency and quality*

The traditional paradigm of prepublication evaluation, most often on the basis of anonymity, has become largely criticized by the scientific community. It can prevent, in a discretionary manner, the sharing of significant results.

This prepublication evaluation is particularly blatant within the medical sphere, where the non-publication of some results could have especially harmful consequences[10].

Faced with this observation, more and more platforms are turning toward open peer review, opening publication review to a large number or even indeed to the entire research community.

8 http://discreteanalysisjournal.com/.
9 http://www.nature.com/news/leading-mathematician-launches-arxiv-overlay-journal-1.18351 [consulted on 18th November 2015].
10 For example, see http://blog.scielo.org/en/2015/08/12/unpublished-results-from-clinical-trials-distort-medical-research/ [which was consulted on 18th November 2015].

The publisher Copernicus[11] (which has produced around 30 jorunals), the *British Medical Journal*[12] and even the platform *F1000Research*[13] have all used this system, where reviews are open to the entire scientific community. The objective is to improve transparency and ultimately publication and discussion quality, by diminishing the risks of researcher misconduct (which might include plagiarism and falsification of data).

9.2. Two main objectives: accelerating knowledge sharing and promoting scientific collaboration

9.2.1. *Accelerating knowledge sharing*

One of the common objectives of the emerging forms of scientific publication is the reduction in publication deadlines and thus the improvement of knowledge sharing.

In the traditional publishing model, it can take up to 18 months between article submission and publication, owing to versions being sent back and forth between the publisher, the author and those reviewing the article.

With models operating using the preprint system (it is thus the case with PeerJ and overlay journals which have already been mentioned), research results are already accessible from the depositary by the author. The results might therefore be immediately reusable, quoted, and if necessary corrected, improving the reuse of research results and the scientific reactivity. In this case, preprint acts as a scientific accelerator.

9.2.2. *Promoting scientific collaboration: academic social networks*

The immediate availability of scientific results and open peer review favors exchange of information between researchers.

---

11 See the page dedicated to participatory peer review: http://publications.copernicus.org/services/public_peer_review.html.
12 See BMJ Open, based upon the operation of open peer review: http://bmjopen.bmj.com/.
13 For information on the publication process of F1000Research, see: http://f1000research.com/about.

This is also the objective of academic social networks, which have witnessed a significant boom in recent years. In May 2015, *Academia.edu* had more than 21.5 million subscribers (compared to 7.5 million in February 2014), *ResearchGate* more than 6 million (compared to around 3 million a year earlier), and many more whose subscriber numbers are lagging significantly further behind. An example might be *MyScienceWork*[14] with around 75,000 subscribers[15].

According to a study of the Copernicus consortium in 2014[16], 71% of French researchers were present on social networks in 2014 (considering both so-called "general public" networks and professional networks). The main reasons quoted for this use were online presence and the ability for contact and exchange of information which flows from it, the possibility of encountering peers, and lastly that of publishing content.

9.3. The need for new analytical tools and the risk of reprivatization of scientific knowledge

9.3.1. *Increase in data and the weakness of indicators: the need for new analytical tools*

9.3.1.1. *"Lost science" and the loss of STI: the responses of scientific production*

So-called "lost science" and the loss of STI online, explained above, are major issues for scientific production. Some emerging forms of scientific publication tried to provide a response to these issues. This is the case of mega-journals, which aim to reduce the quantity of lost science.

---

14 https://www.mysciencework.com/.
15 "Données recueillies" (this translates as "Data Gathered") by A. Bouchard. See: http://urfistinfo.hypotheses.org/2896 [consulted on 12th November 2015].
16 *Réseaux sociaux de la recherche et Open Access – Perception des chercheurs français* [This translates as "Research and Open Access Networks – Perceptions of French Researchers"] – November 2014, available at http://couperin.org/images/stories/openaire/Couperin_RDSR-OA_CARIST_20141124.pdf [consulted on 12th November 2015].

The review *PLoS One*[17], launched in 2006, was a pioneer in this sphere. Considering that reviewing the importance of an article came down its readers, it restricted article review to a single study of scientific rigor rather than a review of the potential significance for readers and the resulting impact factor.

It thus publishes articles stemming from all scientific domains and particularly studies showing negative results or describing methods and which could not be published in traditional journals. *PLoS One* was later copied by all major publishing houses which launched their own mega-journals[18].

9.3.2. *The need for new analytical tools*

Without discrimination on the grounds of theme or journal type, other than those focusing on scientific method, can mega-journals still be considered as journals? Do they not compare more closely to documentary archives?

The emergence of social networks and mega-journals, once again, evokes the need to have analytical tools available allowing optimization of the development of research results and therefore innovation. Yet, current usage of bibliometric indicators such as the impact factor (based upon the average number of quotations and references) as a means of judging scientific excellence in scientific production seems a very fragile mechanism. It is important, indeed, to distinguish a quantitative review from a qualitative review of scientific works.

Moreover, current indicators remain highly heterogeneous, as much within the area of study as in their operation. In addition, analytical tools (specifically relating to content) which are standardized and brought into widespread use still remain to be developed.

_____

17 http://journals.plos.org/plosone/.
18 *Nature* launched its mega-review *Scientific Reports* in 2011, Springer its publication *GigaScience* in 2012, and Elsevier its publication *Heliyon* in 2015.

9.4. The absence of the usage doctrine and the risk of reprivatization of science: the case of social networks

9.4.1. *Academic social networks and major publishing houses: are they undergoing the same struggle?*

Although emerging forms of scientific publication bear within themselves numerous advantages, the absence of stabilization in using academic social networks does, however, present new risks. We indeed note that some academic social networks have very similar practices to those of major publishing houses which researchers are trying hard to avoid, by using these new forms of knowledge sharing.

In a note published in May 2015 on UrfistInfo[19], the URFIST network (Unités Régionales de Formation à l'Information Scientifique et Technique[20]), Aline Bouchard thus cited the case of the network MyScienceWork. First centered upon *open access*, this network was established in 2014 as a partnership with Elsevier to supply its subscribing researchers with access to the *ScienceDirect* catalog[21], increasing the visibility of the social network and the impact factor of Elsevier publications simultaneously.

On social networks, as elsewhere, it therefore seems that the objective remains to appear as an inevitable actor in the scientific production process. Networks, as with publishers, aim to offer the maximum tools used by the researcher when working (for example, research tools, contact tools, knowledge sharing tools and other devices). This is done so as to freely gather the fruits of one's labors thereafter.

9.4.2. *The risk of a loss of benchmarks*

While the number of publications shared on academic social networks increases continually, the issue of a possible loss of benchmarks arises in an increasingly marked way.

---

19 A. Bouchard, "Où en est-on des réseaux sociaux académiques? " [This translates as "Where are we with academic social networks?"], available at: http://urfistinfo.hypotheses. org/2896 [consulted on 18th November 2015].
20 This translates as "Regional Training Units in Scientific and Technical Information".
21 http://www.sciencedirect.com/.

A lack of training around self-publication causes some researchers to use social networks along with open archives, e.g. HAL or arXiv, and post articles there. This poses the question of sustained access to the publication of results stemming from research, when this scientific production is placed in the hands of private actors who are able at any time to restrict access to content, via a subscription or pay-per-view model, for example.

This tendency to use networks rather than open archives is further strengthened by the better visibility offered by the former, which are often better optimized on search engines. Finally, as with social networks intended for the general public, the subject of ownership of data placed online by users, and the risk of data capture by a hosting platform, remains a prime issue.

When all is said and done, although new forms of scientific publication allow for optimized sharing and maximum knowledge sharing, they do, however, present new risks. These imply a level of awareness to be raised among the research community to profit from digital assets without endangering the objective of a science which becomes increasingly open.

The Geopolitics of Science

Francis André, a research engineer at the CNRS, distinguishes four major scientific historical periods[1]. A thousand years ago, an era of experimental science took place which was concerned with describing natural phenomena. More recent centuries have seen eras of theoretical science being major theories, mirroring Newton. In recent decades, a mathematical science modeling complex phenomenon has arisen. Now, Francis André sees within modern science a turning point. This translates as "European Organization for Nuclear Researchent" of science through data study. Jim Gray labels this as "the fourth paradigm of research"[2].

The issue is as follows: the significance of data is both in its sharing and reuse, within a dynamic where research feeds research, in particular within fundamental research.

The challenge resides within the necessity to construct this new way of "producing directly from science" within the existing model, where the patent remains the primary tool and shield for manufacturers. Yet, this latter is considered to grind innovation to a halt.

The tendency is as follows. With the explosion of communication between laboratories and collaborations between public and privately-funded

---

1 According to Jim Gray: Jim Gray, Alex Szalay, eScience: The Next Decade Will Be Exciting, Talk@ETH, Zurich 29th May 2006.
2 Jim Gray, Alex Szalay, eScience: The Next Decade Will Be Exciting, Talk@ETH, Zurich, 29th May 2006.

research, we see a certain willingness to bring intellectual property within an international framework.

This evolution toward "the fourth paradigm of research" is characterized by the convergence of operational structures.

10.1. National convergent research models

Although each country developed different research structures over the course of time, globalization and the communications explosion led various models to evolve in the same direction.

10.1.1. *The United States and sector interpenetration*

Although American public research is highly productive, private research in the United States has largely influenced other countries.

Private American research is characterized by its dual nature, and is mainly organized within "collaboration programs" between universities and businesses, at the heart of geographically situated and identifiable places, such as those found around MIT or Stanford University (Silicon Valley).

The main stimulus of this model is the competition within the market. It results in the phenomenal production of private research, of which the main players are large transnational firms.

One of the most striking examples is Google, which is poised to launch itself on the already flooded automobile market by penetrating the sphere of automatic cars. This is due to the Google Car innovation.

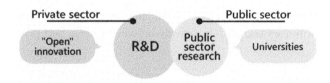

Figure 10.1. *The US and inter-penetration of sectors*

10.1.1.1. *The other "French exception": research*

In France, it is, in fact, public research which has had a greater influence on how French scientists work. The state is a major player in scientific research activities.

According to a 2008 Senate report[3], "the two peculiarities of French research are, on the one hand, the existence of the CNRS and, on the other hand, the civil servant status of the large majority of researchers."

There are several types of public institutions responsible for framing, supporting and financing research.

On the one hand, there are *Etablissements Publics à caractère Scientifique, Culturel et Professionnel* (EPSCP)[4], which are responsible for training young researchers and students. Among them, are universities, some *grandes écoles*, for example the ENS (École Normale Supérieure), and some engineering schools.

On the other hand, there are the *Etablissements Publics à caractère Scientifique et Technologique* (EPST)[5]. The most symbolic is the CNRS, which has the peculiarity of being pluri-disciplinary. The other institutions have particular specialisms (for example INED (*Institute National d'Etudes Démographic*[6]) in demographic research, INSERM (*Institut de la Santé et de la Recherche Médicale*[7]) in medicine). Finally the *Etablissements Publics à caractère Industriel et Commercial* (EPIC)[8], such as the Atomic Energy Commission, or the *l'Institut de Radioprotection et de Sûreté Nucléaire*[9], which have a management and regulatory role.

---

3 Recherche et innovation en France : surmonter nos handicaps au service de la croissance, rapport du Sénat, 2008. (This translates to "Research and Innovation in France: Overcoming our Handicaps in the service of Growth, Report by the Senate, 2008").
4 This translates to "Scientific, Cultural and Professional Public Institutions".
5 This translates to "Scientific and Technology Public Institutions".
6 This translates to "National Institute for Demographic Studies".
7 This translates to the "French Institute of Health and Medical Research".
8 This translates to "Industrial and Commercial Public Institutes".
9 This translates to the "Institute of Radioprotection and Nuclear Safety".

In 2004, a reform led by the *Comité Interministériel d'Aménagement et de Développement du Territoire*[10] put in place competitiveness poles, based on the American models of cooperation areas. The Government then created the *Agence Nationale de la Recherche*[11].

10.1.2. *China: a hybrid model*

The Organic Research Center in China is within the Chinese Academy of Sciences[12]. This academy depends upon the State Council with its headquarters in Peking.

It is made up of five departments. Unlike the American or French models, it focuses uniquely upon pure sciences: mathematics, physics, chemistry, biology and "technology", which groups together computer sciences and robotics research.

It is present in 11 major Chinese urban centers, oversees 84 institutes, the University of Science and Technology in Hefei, four documentation centers, three technological support centers and two publishing centers. This last point is of paramount importance, given the power of global scientific publishers.

The Chinese Academy of Sciences is behind the creation of more than 430 businesses, of which eight are quoted on one of China's two stock exchanges, to increase the value of research results.

Thus, the American model of "cooperation areas" has been expanded here with, on the one hand, industry and research and development, and on the other hand, public research within universities and institutes.

What are the modes of data transfer between these national blocks? How is scientific product circulation organized?

---

10 This translates to the "Inter-ministerial Territorial Planning and Development Committee".
11 This translates to the "National Agency for Research".
12 http://english.cas.cn/.

10.2. Science is a source of international cooperation

10.2.1. *The European Union: a laboratory for joint scientific projects*

The European Union (EU), as a group of states collaborating across all spheres, is in a unique position. Scientific research is naturally a source of collaboration between EU member states. In 2000, the European Commission created the European Research Area (ERA).

The charter of the ERA, which arose voluntarily, was oriented toward industrial and commercial development of research results for competitiveness, innovation and opening up the research labor market for researchers. It organizes, in greater depth, the partnership between public research and industry.

Moreover, this charter seeks to "optimize the circulation and transfer of scientific information, particularly by digital means and a larger and quicker access to publications and scientific data"[13], which is of greater interest to us.

Indeed, for the last 10 years or so, we have been observing a global movement, which seeks to organize cross-cooperation between states, but equally to develop "open science", so that researchers might find private sector science applications.

10.2.1.1. *CERN as a model of cooperation*

The *Centre Européen pour la Recherche Nucléaire*[14] (CERN), celebrated for its particle accelerator, is the result of a project which groups together 21 member states, through the medium of a highly specific cooperation.

Indeed, it is geographically spread over two countries and scientifically across 21 states – of which some are not part of the EU but, however, participate in the ERA. It is the case of Switzerland, upon the territory of which part of the particle accelerator is located, but also of Norway, Iceland, Israel, Macedonia and Turkey.

---

13 http://www.enseignementsup-recherche.gouv.fr/pid24889-cid56014/presentation-de-l-e.e.r.html
14 http://home.cern/fr – this translates to the "European Organization for Nuclear Research".

The UNESCO participates in the project financing. Moreover, several states have the status of "observers" in CERN research. These are India, Japan, Russia and the United States. Finally, 29 countries are "occasional participants" in the work of CERN.

CERN is therefore an extraordinary example of scientific cooperation. European in origin, it is open to all countries close to the EU and also to international institutions.

As regards intellectual property, CERN is a particular good example. Moreover, it was there that Tim Berners-Lee developed the Internet. He chose to let this technology filter through as Creative Commons technology. His idea was to produce a single and unique integrated information tool instead of several such tools coexisting together.

CERN's intellectual protection policy follows this pathway.

Fundamental research is, in essence, open in nature. Member states involved in CERN decided to make intellectual property available to all of their research centers.

CERN also has a technology transfer office which seeks to favor the development of technological innovation based upon CERN research. The institute has chosen the development pathway, a balanced choice through the use of Creative Commons licenses.

The partnership SCOAP3[15] brings together 40 countries and publishes, in real time, the results of CERN. It does so in cooperation with major international publishers, under specific publication conditions.

With the rules on copyright being fairly rigorous, an embargo is applied to scientific results corresponding to publisher remuneration. For several months, publishers circulate these results to their advantage. During this time, they are not accessible and generate value.

This plan is fairly unusual, as short-term profit remains sufficient for the layman to trade in the given innovation and derive a market advantage. SCOAP3 seeks to minimize this "winner takes all" phenomenon.

---

15 https://scoap3.org/.

The embargo system in the short term is of unique benefit to the publisher. SCOAP3 breaks away from this logic. All research results produced at CERN are immediately accessible (uniquely) to all CERN researchers.

CERN advances to publishers the right known in law as the article processing charge (APC). This is around US$2,500.00 per article, which corresponds to relinquishing the publisher embargo, for the relevant article, and the right to publish via open access then begins. All of the articles produced by CERN are subject to agreements which permit the use of the results in consideration of the payment of an APC.

The objective is to realize knowledge sharing before patenting kicks in. Within the OECD countries, intellectual property develops upstream of patents and competes with them. The research industry seeks highly controlled sharing, between the realms of private law and public law. SCOAP3 is thus a highly accomplished example of this.

The major issue with SCOAP3 is to identify cooperations derived from open access and necessitate the activation of a new so-called "sharing layer".

It is not sufficient to share the results. It is also necessary to allow open access to metadata (this is information about information, or how the result is produced), as well as peer-review comments. Indeed, all scientists comment and follow what happens around them, which serves to create a new value chain. We may imagine an open access arrangement consisting of tracks and metadata, over which the public research industry may be overlaid.

This networking may be illustrated by Paperscape[16], mapping software for scientific productions according to their popularity, that is to say how frequently they are cited in other papers. Indeed, the scientific and industrial value particularly resides in the knowledge and who is interested in what knowledge!

Thus CERN, as with all collective multi-entity projects, seeks to offer open access for everything it produces for its relevant players. After all, it should seek to increase the value of the results of its studies to remain viable.

---

16 http://paperscape.org/.

10.3. International scientific cooperation is accelerating

The increase in information exchange within the international scientific community takes places using several methods. These may take the form of spontaneous and disseminated relationships between laboratories, teams and researchers or institutional and political approaches between states.

In any event, the crux of the matter is the Internet and the sharing of electronic data. We can distinguish two scientific results spheres among data exchanges:

The first is the acknowledged sphere of the so-called "common good": principally research in the climate and health sphere, partly managed and financed by, for example, UNESCO, the WHO (the World Health Organization) or the IPCC (the Intergovernment Panel on Climate Change).

The second sphere is one likely to release commercial profits. We can acknowledge that scientific research products enter this category due to several indicators:

– The quantity of patents including transfers of technology, brands or designs, engineering services or even industrial R&D. The number of patents filed is constantly increasing within the OECD, in particular, as regards ICT (Information Technology and Telecommunications) or biotechnologies (leading industries with high added value).

– The technological balance of payments. This is an indicator of international technology transfers. The global volume of the technological balance of payments is constantly increasing. Defined by the OECD as the "primary form of technological dissemination", the technological balance of payments corresponds to commercial exchange, which, of itself, has value and therefore is not free.

We thus observe that there is a tendency toward the expansion of scientific exchanges. Although forms of international cooperation are emerging in a very promising way such as, for example, CERN, the market in this sphere remains highly evident.

Copyright Serving the Market

In March 2014, the World Intellectual Property Organization (WIPO) reported a "record increase in international patent applications filed in 2013, the main drivers being the U.S. and China"[1].

A patent offers an exclusive right over an invention and permits its owner to decide how the invention is used by a third party, even if simply to deprive them of it. The proliferation of patents throughout large global economies shows a very particular parallel market, which makes it possible to gather royalties for the use of patent content.

Figure 11.1 shows the significance of the economics of intellectual property rights. It may also raise doubts of an erosion of the monopoly of knowledge represented by the United States.

Indeed, compared to payment totals exceeding 42 billion dollars, the United States received more than 130 billion dollars in 2014 in commission for intellectual property rights. In comparison, China pays 21 billion dollars in intellectual property rights but only received 886 million dollars for the use of such rights[2].

---

1 "Record increase in international patent applications in 2013 driven by the U.S. and China", Press release, WIPO, Geneva, 13 March 2014, available at: http://www.wipo.int/pressroom/fr/articles/2014/article_0002.html.
2 Consult the graph in: "Commission for the use of intellectual property, payments (balance-of-payments, current $US values)", Data, World Bank, available at: http://donnees.banquemondiale.org/indicateur/BM.GSR.ROYL.CD/countries/1W-EU-US-CN?display=graph.

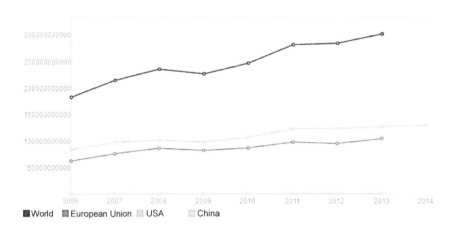

Figure 11.1. *Total commissions for the use of intellectual property, returned (in $US) from the EU, the United States, China and the world between 2006 and 2013*[3]

Yet, it seems that in seeking the protection of artistic or inventor expression, the current trend is toward intellectual property being treated as a commodity.

In England, the first laws relating to copyright appeared during the 18th Century, where the Statute of Anne dated 1710 made it possible to place the work at the sole disposal of its author forbidding its appropriation by printers.

Beaumarchais, who founded the first author's society, later introduced into France the concept of non-pecuniary attributes of copyright. Under this concept, the author has a right of authorship and is in a position to demand that the integrity of his work be respected. These pillars of law put a definitive end to author anonymity and are thereafter supplemented by laws which are increasingly complicating the meaning of intellectual property and its related rights. The French law of the 11th March 1957 even introduced pecuniary rights for the author and his heirs who should receive royalties for both reproduction and representation of their works.

---

3 The data and the graph are extracted from the World Bank website http://donnees. banquemondiale.org/indicateur/BX.GSR.ROYL.CD/countries/1W-EU-US-CN?display=graph.

Finally, on the international scale, a system creating intellectual property laws was developed.

Within the Convention which the WIPO instituted in 1967, laws relating to intellectual property ultimately applied for the following items:

– "literary, artistic and scientific works;

– performers interpretations and artists' recordings, phonograms and broadcasts;

– inventions within all spheres of human activity;

– scientific discoveries;

– designs and industrial designs;

– trademarks, trade names and service marks, as well as commercial names and trade names;

– protection against unfair competition; and

– all other rights pertaining to intellectual activity within industrial, scientific, literary and artistic spheres".[4]

Enlarging the scope of literary and artistic property to that of industrial property demands harmonization on a global scale. The latter is absorbed by international organizations such as the WIPO and the European Union.

For example, the 2001 European Copyright Directive was transposed into French law by the *DAVSI* law (the *loi sur le Droit d'Auteur et les Droits Voisins dans la Société de l'Information*)[5] of 2006, which brings into law Digital Rights Management (DRM), which are the shackles on information technology, which drastically restrict the previously widespread use of physical media such as CD-ROMs or DVDs by, for example, private copying.

The law develops and frames Web uses increasingly harshly. In 2009, the Hadopi laws instigated Internet access surveillance and the graduated response to visiting illegal upload websites. Simultaneously, the limitation of

---

4 "Understanding industrial property", WIPO Publication No 895(F), WIPO URL: http://www.wipo.int/edocs/pubdocs/fr/intproperty/895/wipo_pub_895.pdf.
5 This translates into English as the "law on authors' rights and related rights in the information society".

the public sphere is subject to debate. We may take the American examples with the Copyright Act (1976) and the Copyright Term Extension Act (1998), which extended, one by one, copyright protection up to 120 years.

These laws, which appear to be national laws, are in fact applicable outside of their jurisdictions with the signature of bilateral treaties, implying the adoption of intellectual property laws.

In conclusion, knowledge constitutes an undeniable economic development driver. However, simultaneously, they are subject to an enclosure phenomenon as a result of their privatization. Within this new model, we can therefore conclude with the persistence of economic and informational monopolies on an international scale.

PART 3

Enhancement:
Knowledge Rights and Public Policies
in the Wake of Digital Technology

Legal Protection of Scientific Research Results in the Humanities and Social Sciences

12.1. Different legal protections for different kinds of science

In the chapter on legal systems, it is necessary to differentiate humanities and social sciences from so-called exact or hard sciences. The outcomes of research in the humanities and social sciences are in fact very different to the results obtained in exact sciences.

To simplify, the hard sciences search for processes, products, or, more broadly, results that could have a material application and which are, for instance, potentially marketable (for example research in chemistry for medicine or the pharmaceutical industry).

The humanities and social sciences operate in a different manner, primarily because the nature of their production, as well as their object of study, are different. It is easy to understand that research results in economics, for example, are not produced in the same way as the latest Apple or Google product is produced.

However, even more noticeable is that the institutional operations of humanities and social sciences are different from those of hard sciences. The vast majority of research in these scientific areas is carried out in universities or in partnerships between universities and businesses[1]. Producing results is

---

1 Some research in hard sciences is also carried out according to this model, but this is a much less significant, even miniscule, part in comparison to humanities and social sciences.

not primarily the outcome of a desire to apply a theory or for field analysis, but it is rather more in line with a logical reasoning for producing knowledge, as well as an institutional logic for peer recognition.

For instance, results in humanities and social sciences belong to the so-called "common good", which does not necessarily abide by economic logic[2]. Indeed, the report on governing digital policies in French territories notes that:

> "The more one contributes to the common good, the less one's use is 'compensated'. Re-usable common good is taken to mean all data which is not of a sensitive nature or personal data which the owner has already agreed to share with institutions or any other actor"[3].

To summarize, it is clear that the nature, means and methods of research, as well as the economic logic in these two areas of scientific research, are different. With this in mind, we will therefore see that the humanities and social sciences have their own means of legal protection which, again, are different from those of hard sciences.

12.2. Why protect?

Researchers may have several reasons for wanting to protect their work. The first, and perhaps the most obvious, is entirely subjective. As an individual, it is understandable that a researcher would wish to remain the sole intellectual property owner of the work he or she had produced.

The second reason is institutional. Research in the humanities and social sciences takes place primarily in academia, which is governed by a system of recognition through articles and publications, and individual or collaborative works.

---

2 To qualify our remarks, the reasoning behind work production in humanities and social sciences is not driven by logic based on economic profit on the part of the researchers themselves. Rather, the practice is different for scientific editors, as the chapter on editors demonstrated.

3 Contribution made by Akim Oural to the report on governing digital policies in French territories (Gouvernance des Politiques Numériques dans les Territoires Mission), available online: http://www.pole-numerique.fr/images/documents/Gouvernance_numerique_rapportAkimOural.pdf.

This production falls within the scope of what is known as peer review[4]. Producing is a way of becoming known in the field, and therefore to (eventually) move on to different positions. In other words, it relates to gaining legitimacy and recognition through writing and obtaining new results (that is new theories, discoveries, means of analysis and so on) in a specific field.

For this reason, recognizing the authorship of the research, as well as effectively protecting it, is important for avoiding "unlawful reappropriation" which is harmful to both the research and the researcher.

The final reason is the final reward of publishing works. We mentioned earlier that the humanities and social sciences are not primarily oriented around economic reasoning and this remains the case; however, it is possible for a researcher in the humanities and social sciences to earn money through their work.

For example, by publishing research, a certain amount of money, corresponding to the author's rights, is paid to him or her as the author of the work. It also falls to the scientific journals and editors to verify the authorship of the content they publish – that is, to play an integral part in the economic and institutional game that structures relationships between researchers and publishers in the humanities and social sciences.

12.3. How to protect

12.3.1. *French law*

We will recall, first and foremost, that all personal production (scientific or artistic) can be protected. The Universal Declaration of Human Rights[5] states in article 27 that:

> "Everyone has the right freely to participate in the cultural life of the community, to enjoy the arts and to share in scientific advancement and its benefits."

---

4 This is when one is judged on his or her work by colleagues in the same field. For more details on this subject, see the definition of the publisher Elsevier – available online: https://www.elsevier.com/reviewers/what-is-peer-review.

5 This Declaration is not legally binding; however, it touches on our subject and ensures that it is considered by other jurisdictions.

"Everyone has the right to the protection of the moral and material interests resulting from any scientific, literary or artistic production of which he is the author."

However, and this is the first truly legal difference between the humanities and social sciences and the hard sciences, scientific production in social sciences cannot be patented: "A patent is an intellectual property title issued to the first depositor (physical or moral person) of an invention[6]".

Written works in the humanities and social sciences have a different legal status, and it is necessary to consult the French Intellectual Property Code to find it. The results of scientific research in the humanities and social sciences are protected by the Intellectual Property Code, under the heading "intellectual work".

Article L112-2 of the Intellectual Property Code:

"The following are considered intellectual works under the Code:

1) Books, booklets and other literary, artistic and scientific written works;

2) Conferences, addresses, sermons, pleas and other works of the same nature;

(...)"

In other words, the law applicable in this case is of "author's rights", although this is nonetheless beset by a certain precariousness; under this law, the author of an intellectual work is in fact the person who puts his name on that work[7].

The French Ministry of Culture has clarified this further: "The author's right protects intellectual works without requiring the author to carry out any

---

6 Translation of the definition given by the French National Scientific Research Council (CNRS) – available online: http://www.cnrs.fr/dire/termes_cles/brevet.htm.
7 This, overall quite moderate, disposition can, however, be strengthened by the measures mentioned earlier, which can prove intellectual ownership and are legally admissible in the event of a dispute.

administrative formality of depositing or prior registration. The rules on legal deposit therefore have no influence on the creation of author's rights".[8]

12.3.2. *Foreign law*

At an international level, other means of protection are possible. The first, and best known, is "copyright", although this is not recognized in France but rather only by Common Law countries (namely, Commonwealth countries and the United States).

Nonetheless, there are some differences between French intellectual property law and copyright.

The French National Scientific Research Council (*Centre national de la recherche scientifique* – CNRS) has listed the differences and shared points in the various provisions of the two systems[9] (Table 12.1).

	Author's right	**English copyright (Copyright Act 1988)**
Protection criteria	Originality of work	idem
Formality	The work is protected without filing formalities being carried out.	idem
Author	Physical person who creates the work. *French law conflates the concepts of author and creator.*	Physical person who creates the work. The editor of the published work is also regarded as the author by law for the typographic presentation. *English law separates these concepts, which results in legal persons being recognized as authors.*

8 Online source: http://www.culture.gouv.fr/culture/infos-pratiques/droits/protection.htm.
9 Online source: https://www.dgdr.cnrs.fr/daj/propriete/droits/Docs/comparatif-auteur-copyright.pdf

Prerogatives	**Moral rights** (non-transferable, impossible to renounce): – right of disclosure, – right of authorship, – right of integrity, – right to reconsider or withdraw. **+ Property rights** (transferable): – right of reproduction, – right to representation, – resale right. *French law gives priority to protecting the author and is centered on the author.*	**Material rights** (transferable): – exclusive right to reproduce or copy the work, – exclusive right to distribute copies or samples of the work to the public, – exclusive right to show, perform, project or distribute the work in public, – exclusive right to broadcast the work or to establish it in a cable distribution service, – exclusive right to adapt the work. **+ Moral rights** (non-transferable, possible to renounce): – right of authorship, – right of integrity of the work, – right to oppose a work being unfairly awarded, – right to disclose or not disclose certain films or photographs. *Copyright is more tied to use of the work, with the author becoming secondary. The copyright is therefore related more to protection of the material rights than the moral rights. The moral rights of the author are limited.*
Duration	**Perpetual moral rights**: The property rights are protected during the author's lifetime and for 70 years after his or her death.	**Perpetual moral rights**: The copyright of literary works lasts for 70 years after the author's death. However, copyright on the typographical presentation of a published edition expires 25 years from the end of the calendar year during which the edition was published for the first time.

Table 12.1. *Comparison of author's rights and English copyright*

However, France has, to some extent, opened its legislation to international law by having integrated "Creative Commons"[10] licenses since 2001.

This production system allows the existence of a protection which could be described as "*à la carte*" or "personalized". Indeed, the author's right is divided into different segments for appropriating the work made available to

---

10 For more detail on the history and integration of Creative Commons, visit: http://www.droit-technologie.org/dossier-186/validite-des-creative-commons-face-au-droit-francais.html.

the public (meaning, put online and therefore made available to a large number of people). This system is much less rigid than French author's right or copyright and, furthermore, it gives the author a choice of methods for the distribution and use of their work in a legal and controlled manner[11].

A series of symbols supplement the "CC" of Creative Commons to declare in a sensible manner the means of protecting work put online. It must also be noted that the Creative Commons licenses are not liable to annulment. Indeed, an author who, wanting to protect his or her work under a CC license, can at any time change the means of protection, or even halt the protection of his or her work under that license, although the author cannot revoke the effect of those licenses on copies already in circulation[12].

12.3.3. *The practical system*

There is in fact a protection system which is not *de facto* effective, but which can have some legal value in cases of plagiarism and confirm the authorship of an intellectual work.

This is the use of a Soleau envelope, a measure implemented by the National Institute of Intellectual Property (*Institut National de la Propriété Industrielle* – INPI)[13], which can contain the blueprints for a technical invention just as easily as the content for research in the humanities and social sciences. Its methods of use are simple: it involves inserting a summary of one's research work and the necessary references to confirm the

---

11 Ever greater numbers of works put online by researchers or groups of researchers are protected with this system.
12 Comment made on the HAL open archives site regarding the means of protection and the operation of Creative Commons licenses (see https://hal.archives-ouvertes.fr/page/questions-juridiques#licences_cc).
13 All the information on this measure can be found on the INPI website: http://www.inpi.fr/fr/enveloppes-soleau.html.

authorship of the scientific work, before closing and sealing the envelope and giving it to the INPI, which will hold it for 5 years (renewable).

The other system, which we will call system D, consists of sending oneself one's work by post using a registered courier with a signature and proof of receipt, with the envelope having been sealed by the courier.

As we have said, the author's right and the intellectual property are *de facto* applicable through the act of creation in itself. These provisions are therefore not a way of strengthening the right of authors in any case, but are rather only precautions to be taken when it is suitable in the event of a dispute brought before the law.

12.4. Protect against whom?

It is good to protect, but it is better to know whom one is protecting one's work against. In the case of research in the humanities and social sciences, it primarily involves protecting oneself against plagiarism, that is against fraudulent copying.

While this may seem childish, plagiarism still continues in the field of research and it is not as harmless as blithely copying what your neighbor has done. It is truly a form of intellectual looting which can occur through works being copied (if the plagiarism is never reported) or a person plagiarizing (if that person is unmasked).

Within a university context, this applies to recognition of the scientific work and its author; its credibility, in short. However, in the legal system, sanctions are applied. To this end, article L122 of the Intellectual Property Code defines the author's right and its fields of application, and articles L331 and L336 define the applicable sanctions in the event of non-compliance with the Intellectual Property Code.

However, more harmful than plagiarism is the fight against the appropriation of results which, according to the Intellectual Property Code, are only to be used by the researcher who supervised their discovery and who is, therefore, their author.

We must nonetheless recall that there are limitations to the author's right, particularly in the humanities and social sciences and their increasing publication on the Internet. We will try to summarize the challenges of these flaws as clearly as possible.

12.5. Changing the challenges of Internet protection

The Internet is an incredible space for sharing knowledge. However, within its abundance of information, it sometimes becomes difficult to find the real author of a theory or quotation, just as it can be easy to neglect to mention the source of a quotation which may supplement a research work.

The Internet is therefore becoming one of the strategic spaces used in an equally effective and precise application of the author's right (in whatever form it may take). Copyrights and Creative Commons licenses are examples of the increasing attention paid to this space in order to apply the law there, and to find a law applicable to the web in particular.

However, the long-term impact of the Internet remains to be seen. It is no longer simply a question of a conversation between intellectual authorship and the author's right, but begins to affect the publication and distribution of scientific knowledge.

Research habits have in fact changed since the arrival of the Internet. It has accustomed us to being able to find and obtain information and data of all kinds, including scientific data and quite often for free. It also provides an excellent opportunity for researchers to reach the scientific community and, potentially, other readers[14] more easily.

It is therefore right that sharing on and through the Internet is added to the concerns about distribution inherent in the humanities and social sciences and the peer review system which structures the field[15]. The Internet is undermining the position of scientific publishers.

Scientific publishers are still important in structuring scientific publishing, but the Internet may perhaps cause the models and contracts

---

14 The Internet clearly makes consulting and researching works simpler than carrying out such tasks in a library.
15 We could see this as the successful confluence of technology and the remainder of the humanist ideals of the Renaissance.

between scientific publishers and authors to be reviewed to create a more open distribution of research data[16].

As we have said, the Internet makes research more visible, both to the scientific community and the general public. The question of ethics therefore continues to arise with increasing importance.

The book *Investigating: with what right? Threats to investigation in the social sciences*[17], for instance, reminds us that the "author's right" is not synonymous with the idea of the scientific author possessing all the rights.

Indeed, respect for the subjects studied (when, for example, we are dealing with singular cases, namely, individuals, with regard to research work in subjects such as sociology) requires respect for the persons working with the researcher.

12.6. Legal obstacles related to the author's right

There are several legal obstacles related to the author's right which must be made known, not for the pleasure of breaking the rules, but rather to know how to utilize them better in scientific works.

France provides a specific exemption for anthologies and quotations, which amounts to more or less the same thing. Indeed, an anthology, insofar as it is a singular format and as it respects the preceding author's rights (that is it indicates the names of the authors whose pieces appear in a given work), appears to be a singular work, additionally protected by its own author's right (that being, as we have said, subject to the applicable author's rights of the texts used).

The other legal obstacle regards quotations, which must be made in due form, especially in a scientific work (the full name of the author and the name of the work, article or source cited, as well as the location and date of publication, must be indicated).

---

16 As we saw in a previous chapter, private scientific publishers have a monopoly of sorts which the Internet could change.
17 Sylvain Laurens, Frédéric Neyart, *Enquêter: de quel droit? Menaces sur l'enquête en sciences sociales*, Éd. du Croquant, 2010.

The legal protection of data and the results of research in the humanities and social sciences is in fact similar to the protection of all intellectual works (artistic, literary or scientific).

We can confirm that this is at once the source of the potential flexibility this protection can have and the precariousness which can affect it. As we have seen, the Internet and current digital policies will certainly bring about changes in the law which governs these protection systems. The Internet is an astonishing space, but a changing one on which the law must base its development.

Development of Knowledge and Public Policies

"Enhancement consists of making knowledge and research skills usable and marketable"[1].

This definition can be simplified as "passing from science to technology and finally to usage".

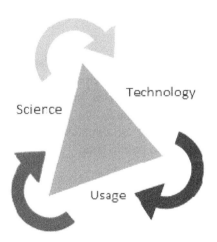

---

1 Translation of the definition given by the French National Evaluation Committee.

13.1. Knowledge enhancement concerns everyone

13.1.1. *An issue in the common interest*

In practice, it is enhancement which enables the passage from the nuclear atom, a product of research, to the production of nuclear energy; from the X-ray to medical radiology; and, through a less direct connection, from quantum physics to the iPhone 6 (with quantum physics having enabled the miniaturization of electronic components).

Research therefore, directly or indirectly, finds applications in society, be they related to medicine, energy, consumption of common goods or anything else. It thereby works toward the common good by improving health, comfort or well-being, or by making daily life easier through new tools.

Furthermore, through the process of "creative destruction" (according to Schumpeter's concept), it enables the creation of new sectors of activity, employment and, therefore, growth.

Investments in knowledge and technologies "will be responsible for close to 25 to 50% of economic growth in industrialized countries", and knowledge contributes to over 50% of their GDP, according to Philippe Busquin[2] in 2001.

By allowing the creation of capital gains for society, the enhancement of knowledge enters into the "public" sphere: it tends to be aimed at the public interest and at improving the general and specific living conditions in society. It is still necessary to have the public policies which facilitate knowledge by surrounding and accompanying it, all in all enabling the transition from private good to public good.

The transition from research (science) to technology (and therefore usage) involves a commercialization of knowledge: where it is profitable for the actors to exploit knowledge.

---

2 Philippe Busquin, Member of the European Commission responsible for research, 6 April 2001 http://europa.eu/rapid/press-release_SPEECH-01-163_fr.htm?locale=FR.

13.1.2. *Multiple actors*

There are multiple actors in the process of enhancing knowledge: researchers and research centers, first of all, who produce this knowledge; investors, both private and public, who enable the existence of this research and its transition to technology; followed by companies, be they SMBs or large groups, which make the results of research marketable; and finally the State, which regulates the framework in which this process takes place. The different actors therefore have specific interests and the role of the public authorities is to maximize the enhancement of knowledge for the benefit of society.

The challenges for the public authorities are therefore to find a fair and practical balance for increasing the efficiency of the industrial and societal benefits of research without restricting or altering the process of production or the dissemination of knowledge.

13.2. What are the public policies for enhancing knowledge?

13.2.1. *The legal frameworks*

The first of the levers of action and managing the public authorities are legal frameworks – legislation. In the field of knowledge, the traditional legal frameworks are the intellectual property rights, defined as the "rights to restriction".

In France, the Intellectual Property Code, created by act no. 92-597 on July 1st 1992, brings together industrial property and literary and artistic property. The latter thereby defines the rights of the author, while the knowledge coming from the hard sciences is protected by patents. This is a key tool in enhancement.

Patents enable the enhancement of knowledge from research in two ways: they provide the knowledge produced with visibility and create incentives for its use and production:

– for buyers of technology (i.e. businesses), patents offer the possibility of gaining access to all products across global R&D, and the transfer of results from public research to private research, with all patent requests being published systematically;

– for those offering technology (researchers and universities), patents encourage specialization in R&D and the selling or licensing of technology, in addition to creating the possibility of raising funds.

Indeed, patents "make the immaterial material": they transform a research work into an industrial property, opening the way to cooperation and partnerships between researchers, investors and businesses.

States organize assistance for industrial and intellectual property in several ways: in France, the National Institute of Intellectual Property (INPI) which encourages assistance for industrial property, including for SMBs and researchers in order to stimulate growth through innovation.

Furthermore, article L.111-1 of the Research Code explicitly states: "*The politics of research and technological development aim to increase knowledge, enhance the results of research, disseminate scientific information (…)*"

In the United States, the Bayh-Dole Act of 1981 promoted the transfer of results from research to industry. It entrusts universities with complete ownership of the results of research, despite the fact that they are financed through federal sources; they are thereby stimulated by being able to benefit from the commercial use of the fruits of research.

13.2.2. *Knowledge enhancement also occurs by allocating funding*

To enable the enhancement of knowledge stemming from research, financial means are required. Various kinds of institutions have been established in European countries and the United States, and by the European Union.

In Germany, the Max Planck Society provides subsidies for transferring research results to the market. It assists the creators of businesses based in the results of research carried out within the Society.

In the United States, the National Sciences Foundation makes funding available for colleges, universities and businesses to stimulate future innovation. It operates through projects being deposited. Other mechanisms have been legally established in the United States for the same purpose, such as the Small Business Innovation Research program, created in 1982 to support innovation in SMBs and SMIs through subsidies. The emphasis is therefore put on the role of universities, which have significant funding for research and innovation (Harvard has 18 billion dollars and MIT 5 billion, made up largely of private donations).

The European Union currently has the Horizon 2020 plan, which proposes continuing support for projects, from "the idea to the marketing stage, and increased support for innovations close to the market". The plan has 80 billion euros for the period between 2014 and 2020.

In France, the Public Investment Bank (Banque Publique d'Investissement) brings public and private funding together to invest in innovations emerging from research and bring them to the market.

Finally, there are financial incentives to encourage the sponsoring of research ("charitable trusts" in the United States, and research levies, exemptions and subsidies in France).

Private funding therefore has an important place in the transfer of knowledge to the market. The State's final lever of action to optimize the enhancement of knowledge, and perhaps the area where the results are most effective, is thus the connections between actors: the State creates the appropriate framework for building cooperation.

13.3. State establishment of connections between actors: a key tool in knowledge enhancement

Connecting the actors involved in knowledge enhancement is to create partnerships between businesses and industries, on the one hand, and universities and research centers, on the other hand, in order to bring research and innovation together. This may take place in a single location, such as in a competitiveness center or incubator.

13.3.1. *Incubators*

In France, there are private and public competitiveness centers and incubators; public incubators are organized and supported by the Ministry of National and Higher Education and Research (*Ministère de l'Education Nationale et Supérieure et de la Recherche* (MENESR)). The first call for a public incubator project occurred in 1990.

The aim of this policy and of making the projects emerging from public research results a reality is to provide support through training and advice, as well as support for research funding.

Through this policy, between 2000 and 2014, 4,000 projects from innovative businesses came into existence in incubators, of which around 41% came from public research and 40% were related to research through collaboration with a public laboratory. These projects led to the creation of almost 2,700 innovative businesses in the same period.

13.3.2. *Competitiveness centers*

Competitiveness centers are themselves the result of an industrial policy which began in 2004. They bring small and large businesses, research laboratories and training establishments, as well as investors, together in one place around a specific topic in the local area, such as for example, the Île de France competitiveness centers PARIS BIOTECH SANTE or AGORANOV, or the PACA ESA BIC in the south of France based around space.

Financial assistance has been proposed by the Special Interministerial Fund (*Fond Unique Interministériel* (FUI)) for the best R&D projects and innovation platforms identified through calls for projects. At the same time, the governance structures of the centers are partially financed through local authorities and businesses. The French National Research Agency (*Agence Nationale de la Recherche* (ANR)), BpiFrance and even the *Caisse des Dépôts* are partners to these centers, guaranteeing links between research, financing and businesses.

In the United States, the well-known example of Silicon Valley shows the effectiveness of competitiveness centers, or "clusters". This area, located in the San Francisco region of California, unites the majority of the computer and Internet giants, including Facebook, Google and Yahoo! It is a hub for new technologies, attracting investments, start-ups and big businesses.

However, this example drives us to question the distribution of roles between private actors and the public authorities in knowledge enhancement; indeed, not only was Silicon Valley originally a private initiative, but private investments also remain largely superior to public ones.

13.4. Comparing the United States and the European Union

We will carry out a comparison between the European and American knowledge enhancement systems in order to highlight the outlines of their operations and summarily compare their respective effectiveness.

13.4.1. *European Union policy*

Since 1983, research and its enhancement in the European Union have been promoted and supervised by the Framework Programme for Research and Development (FPRD) which attempts to standardize the policies of each Member State in this field and, more recently, to create a common area.

In 2000, the European Commission created the European Research Area in order to stimulate scientific excellence, competitivity and innovation by promoting better cooperation and coordination between different actors. It involves implementing a real European "internal market" for research, promoting the movement of researchers, technologies and knowledge and proposing coordination of activities, programs and research policies at Union level.

Within this project, the ERA-NET program enables networking between national and regional R&D programs in order to allow different research funding systems to manage their actions together in a more efficient manner. The ERA thus proposes the supervision of State assistance for research, development and innovation, and aims for a more efficient use of financial initiatives.

Subsequently, the Lisbon summit had the opportunity to confirm the strengthening of these policies, intending to make Europe "the most competitive and most dynamic knowledge economy in the world".

13.4.2. *American policy*

In the United States, knowledge enhancement policies are defined by the "Strategy for American Innovation: driving towards sustainable growth and quality jobs", which establishes the need to invest in the building blocks of American innovation (fundamental research, higher education, infrastructure and ICT) to promote a competitive and open market based on innovation through financial policies and legal measures favorable to innovation and entrepreneurship, and lastly to promote so-called "shortage" technologies in areas deemed national priorities. These areas are clean energy, biotechnologies, nanotechnologies, the high-tech and space industries and health.

While the American giants might immediately come to mind in terms of entrepreneurial success, Europe seems to struggle in many cases to equal or surpass its partner. According to a study carried out by the Graduate Institute for Science and Technology (*Institut des Hautes Etudes pour les Sciences et la Technologie*), the United States has four assets in terms of innovation:

– "a cultural predisposition towards innovation and entrepreneurship: self-confidence and confidence in the future, willingness, acceptance of potential failure, pragmatism, and respect for actions and results;

– the excellence of universities and places of fundamental and applied research;

– the intensity and fluidity of interactions between actors in innovation (in the academic and private sector worlds);

– effective financing mechanisms".

Nonetheless, this comparative effort is restricted by the limited amount of available statistics on the European Union as a whole, despite policy efforts at the European level. This is, in itself, quite revealing: Europe is making limited progress in standardizing its system of research and enhancement of knowledge emerging from research.

14

From Author to Enhancer

Producing knowledge and making it useful to society are primarily the tasks of the author, and subsequently of the enhancer.

Indeed, the author is the person present at the inception of the relevant scientific knowledge. He or she is generally the researcher and can also more broadly represent the university or laboratory to which the researcher belongs.

The term "enhancer", in itself, is a neologism which signifies the business, public institution or private body which is responsible for enhancing scientific knowledge. But what do we mean when we speak about enhancing knowledge?

According to the French National Higher Education Assessment Council (*Conseil national d'évaluation de l'enseignement supérieur*), this process consists of "making the research results, knowledge and skills usable and marketable". Enhancement is therefore the action which connects the research world to the economic, commercial and industrial world, with the aim of literally giving an economic or social value to the results of research through their application.

Without this enhancement process, knowledge would remain purely theoretical. Therefore, to report on enhancement, it is necessary to understand the stages which lead to scientific knowledge, purely theoretical content, acquiring a practical value.

14.1. Enhancing scientific research is a complex process

14.1.1. *Knowledge enhancement may take several forms depending on the objective pursued*

The enhancement of scientific research follows three main objectives and therefore takes three forms.

Financial and commercial enhancement is the most common type of enhancement. It concerns the transformation of an invention into an innovation with the aim of responding to or creating a specific demand. For example, marketing a new medicine through the discovery of a molecule consists of giving an economic value, the price of the medicine, to the discovery of the molecule.

Subsequently, strategic and geostrategic enhancement itself seeks to create innovation, although this is for military, diplomatic and, more generally, defense-related purposes. The space race between the USSR and the United States during the Cold War is a good example of strategic enhancement, as the entire space innovation process was conducted with the aim of increasing the country's power at the international level.

Finally, social enhancement consists of using scientific discoveries with the aim of resolving a more or less defined social problem. Social enhancement generally has access to discoveries in humanities and can have economic benefits at a later time.

14.1.2. *Authors and enhancers are actors in a process which is divided into several stages*

The process of enhancing scientific research is complicated, not only because of the variety of objectives it has to meet, but also because of the diversity of its stages.

In this way, both author and enhancer participate in a more or less shared series of actions. It is possible to bring all of these actions together within a sequential process marked by three main stages.

When enhancing a technology, the first stage is equivalent to enhancement in a restricted sense, in a university setting. This stage is therefore centered on the author; more often than not, it is the author who decides whether he or she wants to enhance his or her invention for economic ends.

During this first phase, the university or laboratory verifies that the invention or discovery does not correspond to an existing patent, before issuing a provisional patent for the invention to protect the intellectual property rights; it will then examine enhancement and transfer strategies by identifying, in particular, businesses that might be interested. However, it must be noted that, in many cases, a business will in fact make a research and development request prior to this stage. Enhancement therefore happens automatically in university environments.

The second stage in the enhancement process, the transfer of technology to the business, is essential as it creates interaction between the author and the enhancer. Frequently, the invention is not completed by the researcher and the business's research teams have to take over. Nevertheless, the invention is the property of the laboratory. Property rights must therefore be transferred from the author to the enhancer, namely, the business, in this instance. The transfer stage is thus essentially a legal one: the owner of the invention (the laboratory) grants new usage rights to the transfer partner (the business).

Generally, these new rights are expressed in a transfer of ownership status: the author of the invention ceases to be the owner in exchange for financial compensation. The technology transfer can also be carried out by transferring a license, a document that defines the invention's methods of use, to the business, thereby giving it the right to use the invention.

Finally, the last stage of the enhancement process falls exclusively within the jurisdiction of the enhancer as it deals with the marketing of the innovation by the business. The business will create a prototype and then, after having tested it, will launch the innovation in accordance with specifications and a marketing plan which have already been determined. The initial invention, through mass production, thereby becomes an innovation placed on the target market.

The sequential plan of scientific enhancement, as described here for a technology, does, however, tend to simplify the enhancement process.

Enhancement is most often not a linear process. The different stages therefore overlap to a greater or lesser extent.

This nonlinearity is particularly important for social enhancement, which is marked by a continuous coming and going from one stage to another and from one actor to another. The enhancement process is therefore not an automatic one.

More precisely, transferring the usage rights of the scientific research product from the author to the enhancer is not automatic as it relies on the good will and agreement of the parties involved.

Faced with this issue that inhibits economic growth and social well-being, the public authorities have increasingly intervened to facilitate the transfer stage of enhancement.

14.2. Scientific research enhancement follows a legislative framework intended to promote innovation

14.2.1. *Public enhancement policies truly came into being in the aftermath of the World War II*

Historically speaking, from the end of the Middle Ages, some States sought to promote innovation by writing the first legislation on intellectual property.

Following that, we had to wait until the positivism of the 18th Century to see the embryos of national innovation services begin to appear.

However, it was not until the aftermath of the World War II that real public policies on research enhancement were implemented in developed countries.

For example, in 1948, the Attlee government in the United Kingdom created the National Research and Development Corporation, an agency designed to transfer inventions and discoveries from British public research laboratories to the private sector in order to stimulate innovation. More precisely, this agency was initially intended to use the products invented and developed by research establishments during the war for defense purposes. This was how the British SRN1a hovercraft came to be marketed in 1953.

14.2.2. *The State attempts to stimulate technology transfers by establishing a specific legislative framework*

In France, several laws have been drafted with the aim of facilitating technology transfers. First, a 1967 act created the National Agency for Enhancement and Research Assistance (*Agence nationale de valorisation et d'aide à la recherché* (ANVAR)), which was tasked with "supporting industrial development and growth to assist innovation, particularly technology, and contribute to developing the results of scientific and technical research".

To fulfill its duty, ANVAR participated in the financing of innovation projects within the framework of service provision contracts. In order to carry out its actions, ANVAR was governed by an 18-member administrative council with six State representatives. However, faced with significant financial difficulties and in the absence of any definition of innovation within its legal framework, ANVAR was replaced in 2005 by OSEO ANVAR, a private business which, while no longer public, has a public service delegation. OSEO ANVAR has the same duties as ANVAR, but they are more specifically focused on small- and medium-sized businesses (SMB) and start-ups, currently considered to be the breeding ground for enhancement.

Furthermore, the Allègre act (an innovation law) of 1999 plays a crucial role in the controlling of enhancement by public authorities as it requires scientific, cultural and professional public establishments to create a structure dedicated to promoting their industrial and commercial activities. This structure is known as the industrial and commercial activities service and thereby enables laboratories to respond to the research and development requests of businesses in an efficient manner.

In June 2009, a decree was added to this act that established a single authorized representative for managing and enhancing scientific research which has been conducted by researchers from different establishments. This decree is decisive as, bearing in mind the resource sharing by different research establishments; it limits the legal difficulties of technology transfers by establishing a single authorized representative among the co-owners of the scientific research product. The business carrying out the enhancement therefore no longer has any need to speak to all research establishments to establish the conditions of transfer, thereby enabling the enhancement of scientific knowledge.

In addition to the laws intended to facilitate the stage for transferring scientific knowledge usage rights, there are a set of legal contracts intended to clarify the relationships between authors and enhancers in order to avoid conflicts of use between these two actors.

Both author and enhancer therefore participate in the process of enhancing scientific knowledge, which is one of the major founding principles of a country's growth and development. Throughout the various enhancement stages, these two actors incorporate the scientific invention into society through its social and commercial realm and in accordance with a specific legislative framework.

Author and enhancer thereby make the scientific inventions accessible and, above all, usable by giving them a practical value. Faced with the possibility of a conflict of use between the actors involved in the enhancement process, the first challenge of public policies is to limit the obstacles to technology transfers and, in that way, stimulate interaction between authors and enhancers.

15

The Right to Knowledge: Moving Toward a Universal Law?

Digital technologies, and the Internet in particular, have become legal challenges in the last few decades as they raise the question of a new approach to knowledge distribution. Indeed, the Internet can be defined by its universality, that is its abstract dimension, existing outside the real world, any clearly defined space and any territory. It is extraterritorial in the first sense of the word: outside all spaces.

Bypassing all national borders, it is beyond all forms of legislation, defined by their national dimensions and therefore by a specific space and population.

In circumventing not only the traditional legal framework, but also the distribution structures for knowledge and goods, the Internet is forced to reconsider the forms acquired and to reinvent and adapt them. According to some, this adaptation would be done within constituencies, that is to say countries, at a national level and in keeping with cultural differences; this was the liberal vision of the Clinton-Gore administration in the 1990s.

It will more likely be carried out in accordance with the universal principle of the Internet through international law, if that itself is adapted to the new formed imposed by the World Wide Web. This was recognized as "public goods" in the United States in February 2015, after a decision taken by the FCC (Federal Communications Commission), responsible for telecommunications, following the Snowden affair. Could this recognition of the universal nature of the Internet lead to international legislation which is global in the sense of universal?

Can knowledge law, through Internet-related legislation, become universal law?

15.1. Unclear regulatory frameworks

15.1.1. *The Internet, a privileged space for soft law expression*

Regardless of whether they are only the beginning, the kinds of regulations which have already appeared for the World Wide Web currently exist in areas related to its use. It involves embryonic forms of rules and of legislation: that which is known as "soft law". This is a type of legislation which lacks the binding nature of the law, in so far as it has little precision, obligation or delegation of power.

This form of legislation has been developed beyond national legal frameworks in the international arena, where States which have the right – through treaties, among other means – have little incentive to restrict themselves voluntarily. Nevertheless, this kind of law has had unprecedented developments, for example by providing organizations with the possibility to act in this legal area. This is the case for the Internet, an area in which, rather than States, it is private organizations, groupings of professionals, which develop a customary form of law. This is effective in that it is carried out by those who are involved in the market, and therefore have sufficient economic power to apply the law.

An example of this is ICANN, the Internet Corporation for Assigned Names and Numbers, created in 1998 by the Clinton administration. The aim of ICANN is to regulate the appropriation of domain names. It relates to a key point in Internet development, as presence on the network is determined by respecting Internet protocol and apportioning a domain name – these are .com, .net, .fr, .us and so on. In 2010, ICANN opened up the field of Internet domain names to internationalized domain names, which allowed the inclusion of longer domain names and the addition of different alphabets, such as the Cyrillic alphabet or Chinese characters.

The legal field of author's rights also has an agreement in the International Confederation of Societies of Authors and Composers (*Confédération Internationale des Sociétés d'Auteurs et de Compositeurs* – CISAC), created in 1926. This is shown through the 2002 Santiago Agreement, which enables the use of works on the Internet to distribute licenses covering several territories. Indeed, given the porous nature of Internet borders, there was an urgent need to develop a global supervisory system: the CIS or Common Information System.

However, this agreement runs counter to European rules as it promotes the creation of national monopolies, prohibited under article 101 of the TFEU on competitivity which also shows the limitations of soft law. The agreement concerns the possibility of "providing commercial users online with a 'one-stop shop' for granting licenses on author's rights encompassing the musical repertoires of all businesses and valid in their territories", an innovation to which the Commission is favorable, although the structure of the agreement itself is not legal.

The Commission in fact considers this agreement to limit the choice of commercial users to the signatory company of the Santiago agreements in their Member State, and thereby to promote the creation of monopolies.

CISAC projects on protecting authors' rights are not, however, limited to the Santiago agreements; the organization has also launched ISAN, the International Standard Audiovisual Number, which has been accepted by ISO, the International Organization for Standardization, another non-governmental organization.

15.1.2. *Setting up international institutional frameworks: the case of data protection*

The flexible legislation standards are not, however, the only current legal frameworks regarding the Internet; the EU also has one of the centers for the universalization of knowledge through new digital networks, with, among others, the 2008 Ljubljana council which recognized the right to freedom of knowledge[1] within the research framework, or European directive 95/46 of 1995 on data protection. More recently, on 9 July 2015, the European Parliament adopted the Reda report on directive 2001 29/EC which encourages "the harmonization of certain aspects of copyright and related rights in the information society" in the Union.

This willingness for harmonization and data protection follows a United Nations initiative focused on the World Wide Web which created working groups such as the World Summit on Information Society (WSIS) in 2003 and its counterpart the Working Group on Internet Governance (WGIG), which both work with the International Telecommunication Union (ITU).

These international organizations aim to "develop the technical standards that ensure networks and technologies seamlessly interconnect"[2] and improve access to the Internet. The final project is to connect everyone on the planet to digital technology to make each person's right to communicate in cyberspace a reality, thereby consecrating the Internet's neutrality principle[3].

In addition, there is the World Summit on the Information Society, which has existed since 2005. This promotes the principle of *multistakeholderism*, which is dialogue between different interest groups on a subject, in this case, States, businesses and international civil society, among others, and a principle taken up by Fadi Chehadé, Chief Executive Officer of ICANN, in his proposal for reforming the institution.

After having been launched in London in 2011, the Global Conference on Cyberspace (GCC) was held last year in The Hague. The 2015 GCC had three major objectives, besides deepening the principles of previous conferences: the taking of concrete actions against immediate threats, such as crime in cyberspace, or taking measures to make the Internet safer; the

---

1 Article 3.4. "COSAC underlines the opportunities that the free movement of knowledge, known as the fifth freedom, could provide for achieving the objectives of the renewed Lisbon strategy", in Conference of Community and European Affairs Committees of Parliaments of the European Union (COSAC), through the contribution adopted by the XXXIX COSAC.
2 http://www.itu.int/en/about/Pages/default.aspx.
3 That is, the equality of all in the face of data processing. All users are able to access the network in its entirety. It relates to one of the Internet's three general principles with openness and interoperability.

development of exchanges and sharing of knowledge and expertise, and searching for a consensus on standards to confront the threats emerging from cyberspace which endanger international stability.

Finally, in 2015, the OECD produced a report on the economic impact of intellectual property rights which highlighted two problems: free access to data within the framework of public–private partnerships and the search for information.

The current legal situation with regard to the Internet is therefore quite vague. It combines flexible standards implemented by independent organizations, trade rules that establish a practice for cyberspace and the beginnings of an international law. It is not possible, in fact, to contemplate an Internet law which would not be universal. The extraterritorial aspect of the Internet is what makes it interesting; what is the use of a connection limited to one area, country or continent? The pitfall affecting legislators is the resistance of national legal systems, the complexity of harmonization which almost makes the State an Internet legislator, and the difficulty which currently has to be overcome.

15.2. Developing legal frameworks related to the Internet is complicated

15.2.1. *The historic development of the Internet occurred without the support of a clear legal framework*

The current situation surrounding digital technology laws is indeed complicated and unique to each country. The reason behind this is the attachment of States to their sovereignty, which manifests itself, among other things, in the legal framework and characteristics of each country, their histories and traditions, as well as in cyberspace itself; this has been able to develop without the need for initial State intervention, with a sufficient expansion base being formed by the cable routes following telephone lines and the "regime of code writers", according to the Lessig formula. The Internet has therefore primarily been an unregulated market, or almost, as was the case with the dot com business prior to the year 2000, a market bubble that popped at the turn of the century.

The harmonization of Internet-related legislation does indeed encounter differences in interests, primarily. This is shown, for example, in the issue of intellectual property in Europe and the USA, where liberal and social beliefs collide between the two areas. In Europe, the question of protecting data is a key, while, in the USA, a more lax approach has been adopted.

15.2.2. *Moving toward an extraterritorial approach to standards?*

This is also the – extreme – case of China, which opposes universal access to knowledge and wishes to regulate the information its citizens can access, with, for example, the aim of securing its regime. However, China is not the only country which has attempted to erect barriers against technology; when the Internet first came onto the scene, Germany also tried to censor pornographic sites, in accordance with its national law.

It required the services of CompuServe, a server which blocked the access of German citizens to certain sites. Under these circumstances, this censure did not have any effect, and CompuServe proposed to ask its users, by mail, to choose whether or not they wanted to restrict their access to certain sites. This is a kind of parental control at a State level. In Germany, these measures remain fragmented and without almost any effect, with any person who wants to connect regardless being able to circumvent the block by reconfiguring the connection. Nonetheless, they remain a nuisance.

In China, the problem is different, with control of transmission cables being carried out at the ground level which makes accessing prohibited sites difficult, but not impossible. By using an American server which recodes the data of sites, it remains possible to connect to Facebook and Google. The problem which arises here is that the will to control comes from a State that chooses to resort to censoring the entire Web, to the extent that the Internet is not a spatial domain. With Internet access being complete – or almost – everywhere, wanting to regulate access to a space leads automatically to wishing to regulate the access of everyone; the problematic request therefore remains the same.

This lack of harmonization between States only makes the need for international legislation clearer; nonetheless, it remains highly problematic as these are the States that must come to an agreement to involve everyone in Internet regulation. The problem is indeed that, even if the Internet remains independent of direct State action, increasing numbers of voices continue to be raised against the control exercised by the United States, particularly after the Snowden affair, which revealed that the NSA collected personal and private data.

So far, it is only Mark Zuckerberg who declared that "the US government has become a threat to the Internet", on 13 March 2014 on Facebook. However, the United States is not alone in exercising indeterminate control over cyberspace; the almost unilateral domination of the GAFA (Google-Apple-Facebook-Amazon) companies also raises questions or even worries, regardless of the recent development of emerging markets putting the balance of the Internet in perspective.

In that regard, China alone has almost as many Internet users as the United States and Europe combined (642–670 million in 2014). Faced with the temptation to split the Internet into as many islands as there are States, and faced with the unacknowledged control of some States on the data circulating in cyberspace, how can the Internet be a universal asset? How can we protect Internet users and promote an international, and therefore universal, legal framework to protect all people and confirm the principle of Internet neutrality?

15.3. Proposals for developing legal frameworks for the Internet

15.3.1. *Proposals which fall within the framework of public or private international law or into new approaches*

How then can we move on from this state of affairs? What kind of international law could govern a field as new as cyberspace and what forms could the standards take? How can we preserve the universality of the Internet while protecting its users?

Several solutions have been contemplated. It has therefore been possible to create a parallel with international environmental law, which considers that, in cases of misdeeds caused by people and with a cross-border impact, the responsibility is borne by the States that did not know how to prevent the event; the problem with this perspective is the return to territoriality. Others, such a J. Malcolm, propose that the Internet be made a common asset in terms of public international law, or in an economic sense, as per A. Bensoussan and R. Fabre. A common asset, in economic terms, is synonymous with a public asset in its use, namely, as a non-rival and non-excludable asset. This concept can be found within the legal framework for a digital republic put forward by A. Lemaire, who wants to make digital technology accessible to all.

However, this concept differs from that which has developed within the framework of international public law, which created the idea of the "common heritage of humanity" or *res communis omnium*, the framework through which territories as different as the Antarctic or space are regulated. The Internet could possibly apply this universal dimension, which could transform it into an asset shared by all and regulated through one of several international treaties; the case remains that an agreement must be found on the standards to be applied. D. C. Menthes proposes that the rules currently applied to the international public domain should be applied to the Internet, and to hold all Web users to the applicable laws in their countries. The question of extraterritoriality and its new definition will therefore eventually be raised – when will extraterritoriality truly exist?

Some advocate the creation of new frameworks for the Internet, as it circumvents all known frameworks. This is, for instance, the initiative taken by Tim Berners-Lee, who drafted a global constitution for the Internet, an Internet Bill of Rights. This places the basic principles of cyberspace above national laws to prevent States modifying them left, right and center, according to the economic and social contexts.

In the same vein, Johnson and Post believe that none of the models in existing international public law can be applied to the Internet, which requires a suitable, and thus new, protocol to be set up. They therefore suggest creating a code on the fundamental principles related to the Internet which would be applied to cybercommunities relatively similar to nation States in the real world, recreating kinds of global villages in cyberspace, and which could even be an organization under the United Nations.

15.3.2. *The absence of Internet territoriality and the obstacles to be overcome*

There are multiple kinds of possible regulations, and there is legislative will pushing for an agreement and regulations through research. What, then, is preventing such projects? Why is there no international agreement on cyberspace, in the same way that there is for the seas?

Numerous problems arise when one considers making the Internet a space regulated by international law. Is it a topic for international public law? Private? Must it be made part of the common heritage of humanity? What will it be before the laws are applied to businesses? To software developers? Should they be taxed according to an international system? Will they remain taxpayers in their countries of origin? How should problems of extraterritoriality[4] be managed? It exists in regard to laws and in regard to people; with international legislation, the agreements must supersede national laws, but with people? If there is a principle in international law relating to the extraterritoriality of citizens, which relies on the *aut dedere aut judicare* (extradite or prosecute) principle, it generally addresses bilateral agreements signed by two States. How, then, can a system be managed at the international level?

It would involve a complete review of the current system, which leaves most things to States. Concerning the extraterritoriality of standards, even if international treaties or customs are theoretically superior to local laws in the majority of countries, there are numerous dual legal systems which only recognize international law once it has been adopted and transposed into national law. The most obvious example is the United Kingdom, where there cannot be an authority higher than Parliament.

To these issues, which a reform of the system could eventually resolve, we add the problem of the legitimacy of public or private international law to take hold of the topic of the Internet, as international public law only theoretically applies to State and international organizations; and that it is international private law that primarily addresses businesses and the individuals residing in different States.

---

4 Extraterritoriality is a principle in international law where a State cedes some of its legal expertise from one territory to another, which therefore opens up the possibility of extending its national powers of fulfilling and creating standards.

If we were to finally abandon law and move on to citizen self-regulation of the Internet, according to the Confucian or customary law model, a system creating a social hierarchy which respects tradition without requiring clear instruments of coercion, would there not be a problem of creating a law for the strongest, or rather a law for the best connected? How can a citizen who does not have knowledge of cyberspace be defended against a hacker with mastery over all of their computer's operations?

The problem of Internet regulation and knowledge access therefore continues to be unresolved. If it is clear that there will not be any national solutions, the creation of a universal law, taken as an international law, will have to surmount numerous challenges before it could be applied, as well as State resistance to market-related issues. It would not only have to overcome varied and wide-ranging legislative obstacles and opposition; it is particularly the choice of a protocol or regulatory method which must be made above all in order to enable values to find their place in cyberspace. One thing which is certain is that cyberspace law must enshrine the general principles of the Web – openness, interoperability and neutrality; "an Internet governance faithful to its values", to paraphrase the Senate[5].

---

5 *L'Europe au secours de l'Internet : démocratiser la gouvernance de l'Internet en s'appuyant sur une ambition politique et industrielle européenne* (Europe coming to the aid of the Internet: democratizing Internet governance by building on a European political and industrial ambition), information report no. 696, 2013–2014.

Governing by Algorithm

In this overview, we will examine the way in which we can use knowledge to govern.

The works of Alain Supiot on governance through numbers have contributed to the emergence of issues surrounding the position of numbers and of physical and mathematical laws in our policies, particularly the impact of these policies on the distribution of work. His works show the importance of quantitative methods in justifying decisions. From a historical and legal perspective, we can date concerns of governance to the 17th Century and the specters of government by machine.

In *Leviathan*, Hobbes offers a perspective of that argument: "For by Art is created that great LEVIATHAN called a COMMON-WEALTH, or STATE, (in latine CIVITAS) which is but an Artificiall Man; though of greater stature and strength than the Naturall, for whose protection and defence it was intended"[1].

There is therefore repetition in the remarks of 21st Century "technologist" authors such as Parag Khanna, who talks about a "generative system of governance which can be designed to provide stability at the same time as positive change"[2]. While the references and the vocabulary have changed, the ideological basis seems to have remained the same.

---

1 Hobbes, Thomas, *Leviathan* (originally published in 1651), Penguin Books, 1981.
2 Khanna, Parag; Khanna, Ayesha, Hybrid Reality: Thriving in the Emerging Human-Technology Civilization, TED Books, 2012.

Nonetheless, there has been a real change in tools and Alain Supiot's cautious mention of algorithms is proof that there is still no work being carried out on the suitability of the policies of the most developed countries with regard to science and technology. How can governance through knowledge really be arranged in the age of digital technology?

Statistics foreshadow algorithmic work and the development of statistics is necessary to it; while algorithms have played an increasing part in decision-making, they can nonetheless provide a useful tool for a redemocratization.

16.1. Statistics that foreshadow algorithms

16.1.1. *The gradual development of statistics*

The ideological roots of statistical work appeared before positivism, in the works of the mechanists of the 17th and 18th Centuries. Returning to the Cartesian concepts of the animal machine, engineers explored mechanization and automation. Jacques Vaucanson, a member of the Academy of Sciences, presented his automated flute at the Saint-Germain fair in 1737. The idea of automation developed in medicine, with Julien Offray de La Mettrie, in his 1748 tract "Man a Machine", supporting a radical monism applied to human beings.

This favorable intellectual ground saw the emergence of rationalist discourse on politics and on the need for statistics as tools of government. Mathematic rationalism aimed for objectivity. In France, the Marquis de Condorcet developed a statistical approach to representative assemblies and juries. The works of Thomas Bayes in England took the theoretical aspects of statistics further. Bayes' theorem is the key tool in predictive statistics, probability and forecasting. It was quickly taken up in medicine in assessing false positives in screening tests.

Alain Desrosières identified Bayes' work as the key turning point in statistics which subsequently enabled the developments, through Gauss and Laplace, which completed Bayes' demonstrations on calculating the probability of known events provoked by unknown causes through inferences on distribution and errors. This solid foundation serves as the basis for a State's entry into studying the field of statistics.

The French General Statistics Office (*Statistique générale de la France*) was established in 1833, but its teams were given few technical means to gather data and did not acquire any real importance before the end of the Third Republic, with the field having remained relatively closed. During the World War II, René Carmille, comptroller general of the French armed forces, set up the system; it was conceived between the two Wars by creating the National Statistical Service (*Service national des Statistiques*), which recruited students of polytechnic schools and was provided with an applied school that would later become the National School of Statistics and Economic Administration (*Ecole nationale de la statistique et de l'administration économique*). The National Statistics Service itself became the INSEE in 1946.

In other countries, we have also seen the institutionalization of statistical and economic studies, endowed with a double legitimacy from both science and the State. Since the 1970s, surveys, demographic studies and price and salary indices have played a leading role in political decision-making and public opinion. The idea of expertise appeared and econometrics asserted itself as the key science.

In this way, the study of governance through numbers is already ubiquitous and calls some people to consider its potential political impact. It was during these years that the concept of automation was born.

16.1.2. *The appearance of automation*

In 1972, Stafford Beer, a major cybernetic theorist, entered into a partnership with auditors in Chile, requesting assistance to build what Salvador Allende, elected in 1970, called "the Chilean path to socialism". Allende's goal was to govern the key industries that had been nationalized in an effective manner. Beer developed a system designed to govern the country which he called Cybersyn, because of cybernetic synergy.

The starting point for this project was that data collection in itself did not allow operational decisions to be taken as the facts resisted aggregation. The idea was to use computing to simulate the consequences of decisions, allowing more effective decision-making through sensors that collect data on key indicators. Chile, however, had neither adequate computational capabilities nor a sufficiently advanced industry to make this system work.

In spite of everything, a control room had been developed which gave Data Feed access to all of a country's economic information in real time. Allende gave Beer the political support necessary to develop such an ambitious project, but he himself was overthrown by Pinochet in 1973, putting a brutal end to this avant-garde project.

Today, algorithms have become part of political decision-making and can be a tool for democracy.

16.2. Algorithmic governance and democratic opportunities

16.2.1. *The importance of algorithms in the decision-making process*

Algorithms illustrate the importance of statistics and data in decision-making. An algorithm is primarily a "general method to resolve a set of problems". It is capable of standardizing the protocol for detecting and resolving a problem by analyzing input and producing output in the form of analysis or a decision. These systems are currently particularly used in the field of surveillance.

Some companies dedicate themselves to analyzing data using algorithms, such as Palantir, one of the NSA's contractors. The surveillance act voted for by French parliamentarians introduced the government to this method of resolving problems. There is indeed a way of delegating politics to machines.

This is also the case in the systems for allocating places in the Post-Baccalaureate Admissions system for French students, which is regulated by a series of algorithms which take into account place of residence, grades, university rankings and the number of applications to carry out an automated allocation. The same system exists for placing teachers in public schools.

There is therefore an inquiry to be conducted on such bodies, which take decisions with highly significant impacts on human lives. Alain Bensoussan refers to the need to create a legal identity for algorithms, just as businesses have a legal identity. The issue is complex, as algorithms are not always distinct and the systems used to monitor terrorist threats, for example, operate by combining several algorithms.

16.2.2. *The democratic importance of algorithms*

The democratic importance of algorithms, then, lies in the political choices which will guide the uses of these systems.

The computing and freedom act of 1978 provides the legal framework. Its article 10 specifies that "No judicial ruling involving a judgment of the behavior of an individual can have as its basis automated processing of personal data intended to assess certain aspects of his or her personality. No other ruling giving rise to legal effects with regard to an individual can be made on the sole basis of automated data processing intended to determine the profile of the relevant party or assess certain aspects of his or her personality". Automatic rulings are removed from normative rulings.

Furthermore, there are other mechanisms which permit the right to review rulings made according to algorithms. The work of the Etalab project, launched in 2011 under the Prime Minister, aims to bring about the open publication of data generated by the State. One of its tasks is to provide the algorithms used by administrations. This is the case of the OpenFisca platform, which allows users to calculate their taxes themselves or to develop applications to calculate their assistance. There is therefore an opportunity for individuals to get hold of State algorithms and examine them critically.

16.2.3. *Moving toward a State platform*

Some believe the State should become a platform by combining algorithmic and open processes. One of the most eagerly anticipated initiatives in this area is the France Connect portal, which will be a single gateway to all digital public services. It is inspired by Tim O'Reilly and his idea of "Government as a Platform".

The objective is to turn the State toward users, its citizens. Henri Verdier and Nicolas Colin have supported this view in "The Time of Plenty" (*"L'Age de la multitude*"). The means to allow intelligent and relevant reuse will mainly be APIs, "contextualized service providers", which are already present in the scientific sphere and use of which must increase in the field of government.

Henri Verdier supports the idea of a hierarchization of data. Some should be completely accessible and reusable, others only accessible through the platform but not reusable, while some should remain internal within administrations. This is because, although citizens request data to assess public actions, administrations remain the primary applicants for the data produced by their colleagues.

The use of algorithms is one the major issues for government in the digital age. Its growing popularity was not created in a void away from technological advances, but from the historic development of the concept of governance which can be progressively measured. Its contemporary uses raise related democratic challenges. The possibility of giving citizens access to these tools exists and is beginning to be used.

The challenge going forward is the political decision which will be made in the choice of legislation adopted in the act for a Digital Republic in France.

Public Data and Science in e-Government

In France, public data are categorized by a legislative framework from the last century, and are supposed to be available upon request[1], just like any document produced by the administration.

Article 1 of act no. 78-753 of 17 July 1978 specifies acceptance of the term: "whatever their date, their place of storage, their form and their medium, documents produced or received, within the framework of their public service work, by the State, or by regional communities, as well as by persons under public law or persons under private law responsible for such work. Such documents include files, reports, studies, summary records, minutes, statistics, directives, instructions, circulars, ministerial notes and responses, correspondence, notices, forecasts and rulings".

The issue of data accessibility is therefore an established one, related to the democratic process, but the development of new information and communication technologies has contributed to increasing and broadening this requirement. The open data movement shows the transition of the obligation to communicate administrative documents upon request toward making all public data available in a precautionary manner and from a point of view of reuse. Such a requirement raises issues in terms of quality and the extent of accessibility of these data, but it also creates significant positive externalities on both the political and economic levels.

---

1 Under some conditions specified in article 4 of the act of 17 July 1978.

This issue of accessibility is also found in science and, in particular, at the public research level; in fact, the latter, financed by public funds, is a "shared asset[2]" and as such should be as widely accessible as possible. The open data and open science movements thus represent the formulation of new demands from civil society, calling for an adaptation of existing public policies, as illustrated in a European Commission recommendation from 2012 requiring States to "define clear policies for the dissemination of and open access to research data resulting from publicly funded research" and ensure that "research data that result from publicly funded research become publicly accessible, usable and re-usable through digital e-infrastructures[3]".

In the face of these new requirements, the development of digital governance seems necessary in order to manage and guide the process, namely, setting up a true e-government. We will first consider the requirements and their foundations before looking at the responses provided.

17.1. Disseminating data and disseminating science: a new requirement

17.1.1. *The openness of public data and the dissemination of science: a democratic requirement?*

The assertion of openness of public data as a priority is not new and has its origins in the democratic requirement of the right to information. Article 15 of the Declaration of Human and Civic Rights specifies that "society has the right to ask a public official for an account of his or her administration". To make public data accessible therefore allows democratic control. While enabling the accessibility of public data strengthens the democratic nature of a society, enabling its reuse increased the possibilities for citizen involvement.

For Simon Chignard, the provision of public data records provides citizens with the opportunity to intensify their participation in public life by developing new services[4]. The openness of public data accordingly falls

---

2 http://www.cpu.fr/actualite/les-donnees-de-la-science-un-bien-commun/.
3 Communication from 17 July 2012 (C(2012)4890) on access to and preservation of scientific information.
4 Simon Chignard, Datanomics : *les nouveaux business models des données* (Datanomics: the new data business models), Éditions FYP.

within a process of improving the relationship between those who govern and those who are governed.

The issue of free access to scientific publications financed by public money is part of a similar problem, with the knowledge belonging to all point. Restraining the time of embragoes is purely and simply a logical sequence in the democratization of the research system: indeed, it permits widespread distribution. This sequence of widespread distribution corresponds to a democratization of the research system. It concerns not only the distribution of publications, but also of databases used by researchers in order to support science.

17.1.2. An economic and social issue

Beyond the democratic stakes, the provision of public data covers an issue of economic and social enhancement. In this respect, we can recall the initiative of the business Home'n'Go which, through data provided by regional authorities, made an interactive map of local taxes[5] to assist clients in choosing their future place of residence. These data were on the servers of different regional authorities, and making it available to the public has enabled the development of a new service of interest to both citizens and potential clients. In Denmark, the provision of databases of GPS addresses has thereby enabled the creation of 62 million Euros worth of profit according to the Danish Enterprise and Construction Authority[6].

The openness of public data is in itself an important economic market insofar as data must be processed and aggregated to be used correctly: there are large differences between making the scanned version of an administrative document available and enabling the reuse of complete data records produced by administrations.

In this respect, public actors need to be assisted in these approaches by outside contributors. In France, since 2011, the start-up Open Data Soft has proposed solutions to public actors to help them open up their data and develop new services.

---

5 https://homengo.com/immobilier/impots-locaux/carte/.
6 Danish Enterprise and Construction Authority, 'The value of Danish address data', 7 July 2010.

The circulation of data produced by administrations or research generates positive externalities for all actors involved, both public and private. Indeed, it allows the sharing of means and therefore a reduction in costs, just as the creation of a synergy when these data are coupled with private data, giving rise to a new "golden triangle of information[7]" according to the formula of Vivek Kundra, former Chief Information Officer (CIO) of the United States.

17.1.3. *Protecting personal data*

The issue of protecting privacy is central to openness, with good e-government having to take such issues into consideration and establish a legal framework that strikes a balance between dissemination and protection.

In the United States, opening up databases that list crimes has led to the appearance of numerous "crime reports"[8] sites, allowing citizens to identify the safest neighborhoods and, conversely, the most dangerous neighborhoods. While the improvement of information can be considered a positive externality, the distribution of the addresses of homes that have already been burglarized poses a problem with regard to privacy. The issue is exactly the same for the data produced by research, and their distribution must take place in accordance with privacy protection standards.

While this example may seem anecdotal, the issue of protecting privacy through e-government has already been raised in European courts. Indeed, while two European regulations place an obligation on member States to publish a list of beneficiaries of European aid allocated to farmers from European funds, the European Court of Justice (ECJ) was requested to give a preliminary ruling on the compliance of this obligation with articles 7 and 8 of the Charter of Fundamental Rights on respecting private and family lives and protecting personal data. In that case, the ECJ ruled that the damage to physical persons was too severe in relation to the need for transparency[9].

---

7 http://techcrunch.com/2015/08/05/government-data-and-the-uber-question/.
8 See crimereports.com.
9 C-92/09 and C-93/09 Volker and Markus Schecke GbR and Hartmut Eifert c/ Land Hessen, ruling of 9 November 2010.

It is therefore not enough either to open up or to allow the reuse of public data, but it is necessary to process data to make it anonymous which requires expertise and management. The project to merge the French Commission for Access to Administrative Data (Commission d'Accès aux Documents Administratifs (CADA)) and the National Commission for Information Technology and Freedoms (Commission Nationale de l'Informatique et des Libertés (CNIL)) can be seen as an illustration of the will of the French government to make progress on this issue.

17.2. Public data in the e-government

If, in the United States, we can consider e-government to have been created by the 1966 adoption of the Freedom of Information Act[10], it is only since 2007, with an amendment of that act through the OPEN Government Act, that the ideas of transparency, governance and availability of public data have been put at the center of public policies across the Atlantic.

In Europe, it was the 2003 directive of the European Parliament[11] on the reuse of public sector information that marked the beginning of the establishment of new public policies due to changes in law.

In France, the government took hold of this new issue by creating the Etalab project, associated with the General Secretariat for the Modernization of Public Action (Secrétariat Général pour la Modernisation de l'Action Publique (SGMAP)), which aims to guide policy for making public data open and shareable. It is specifically responsible for the interministerial portal data.gouv.fr, bringing together all data made publicly available by the State, public institutions, regional authorities and entities in public and private law responsible for fulfilling a public service function. Created by a Prime Ministerial circular[12], this ruling provides for the integration of the principle of free reuse of public data and the formalization of a true e-government process in France.

---

10 http://www.foia.gov/.

11 Directive 2003/98/EC of the European Parliament and of the Council of 17 November 2003 on the re-use of public sector information.

12 Circular of 26 May 2011 on the creation of a single State portal for public information 'data.gouv.fr' through the Etalab project and the application of measures regulating the law on re-use of public information.

Similarly, in April 2014, France joined the Open Government Partnership, a multilateral partnership with the objective of promoting the use of new information and communication technologies in order to combat corruption and set up more transparent and participatory governments. This movement, which, in 2015, united 65 countries, aims to promote a model of e-government across the world, with each country having to produce a national action plan to advance transparency and openness in public action. The implementation of the biennial plans is then evaluated by an independent mechanism in line with the partnership. This international approach in support of a new e-government illustrates the challenge presented by the opening up of public data, but particularly of the mastery of this process and others to follow, or, put another way, the development of a digital governance.

The creation of the post of General Data Administrator (Administrateur Général des Données (AGD))[13], along the lines of the American Chief Data Officer (CDO), completes this approach by implementing a body for managing and governing State data. If *a priori* the AGD is not intended to participate in opening up public data, it plays an important role in upstream data processing and in the control that the State has over its own data. The challenge is therefore not only the openness of data but also its control: considering and establishing e-government is to use new technological tools primarily to include citizens in the workings of democracy and increase its transparency.

The draft act for a digital Republic proposed by Axelle Lemaire, Secretary of State for Digital Technology, by suggesting the openness of public data by default and the distribution of data of economic, social or environmental interest[14], marks the beginning of a new period of openness. Without setting a standard for data distribution, it requires there to be an "open and easily reusable standard", and this draft act therefore proposes a form of openness in support of open data, while letting the administration take charge insofar as any deadline requirements for implementation are specified or the issue of public data for pay is addressed. Within the

---

13 Decree no. 2014-1050 of 16 September 2014 establishing a General Data Administrator.
14 http://www.republique-numerique.fr/project/projet-de-loi-numerique/step/projet-de-loi-adopte-par-le-conseil-des-ministres.

e-government framework, it concerns the move to a controlled openness in order to respond to these new challenges.

17.3. Science within e-government

With regard to science, the role of e-government can be found in the management and supervisory functions for the distribution of data produced through public research. Free access and the opportunity to use these data must exist within a secure and reliable framework.

In the discussions which took place at the Open Access event on universalizing open access to research results (24 and 25 January 2013), Geneviève Fioraso, then French Minister for Higher Education and Research, presented the principle and the challenges of Open Science by stating that, "scientific information is a shared asset which should be available to all"[15].

Since then, the French government has been committed to developing a platform dedicated to open science which aims to be the database of databases, or, in other words, to propose a single access point for all scientific data in the world.

This project is the ISTEX project (Initiative for Excellence of Scientific and Technical Information – Initiative d'excellence de l'information Scientifique et Technique), and its primary duty is to enable resource sharing through a system of national licenses. Instead of seeing every individual establishment subscribe to the resources of different publishers, this system is based on a single contract between France and a publisher which concerns a set of resources accessible in a specific area. The first part of this program therefore consists of "a voluntarist and widespread policy for the centralized procurement of scientific archives in the form of national licenses"[16], producing significant economies of scale and moving toward breaking down barriers in research. Endowed with 60 million Euros to build a platform and obtain archives, this project will allow equal access to scientific information for the entire French research community.

---

15 http://www.enseignementsup-recherche.gouv.fr/cid66992/discours-de-genevieve-fioraso-lors-des-5e-journees-open-access.html.
16 https://www.actualitte.com/article/monde-edition/le-projet-istex-pour-renforcer-la-recherche-francaise/35817.

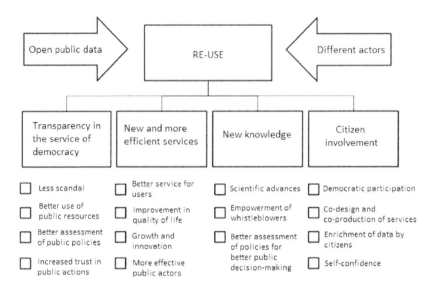

Figure 17.1. *The use of data (according to Daniel Kaplan:*
http://www.internetactu.net/ 2010/11/09/louverture-des-donnees-
publiques-et-apres/)

Surveillance, *Sousveillance*, Improper Capturing

If the value of science can be defined as the combination of the results obtained and the sharing of those results, it is remarkable that the latter is currently the field of numerous debates and experiments, within a discerning economic and legal framework, and involves a plethora of variables.

Indeed, results sharing raises the subsequent question of the ownership of these results and the data obtained. In France, this modality is partially regulated by the intellectual property law, which was codified in 1992[1] and is a precisely defined law with a double dimension of moral and patrimonial knowledge.

In addition, the acceleration of means of distributing and communicating knowledge raise a significant contextual factor: the development of open access applied to science, the growth of user-generated content and even the increasing importance of Application Programming Interfaces (API) is blowing up the traditional legal frameworks, with property thereby becoming a matter of speed.

Finally, the expansion of the surveillance of data and results is the subject of a question at the heart of our analysis: anti-plagiarism algorithms (Urkund[2] at Sciences Po university, for example); the development of

---

1 https://www.legifrance.gouv.fr/affichCode.do?cidTexte=LEGITEXT000006069414.
2 http://www.sciencespo.fr/ressources-numeriques/content/le-systeme-anti-plagiat-urkund.

sousveillance[3], that is the uncontrolled reuse of information through, among other means, social media; improper capturing and, through intellectual property law and the mandatory use of API, there are just as many parts to the complex problem of fluctuation between openness and data protection. This is particularly true as it deals with a changing reality; as Jean-Gabriel Ganascia observed, we are moving from the "Panopticon"[4] era, conceived by Jeremy Bentham, to the "Catopticon"[5], leading to the idea of an underlying monitoring, where each party in a given society observes and monitors each other, raising the issue of the elusiveness of data ownership.

It is therefore urgent to reflect on speed discrepancy, between legal frameworks on the one hand, and uses changing ever more quickly on the other hand, making traditional law an unsuitable tool for regulating property-related events.

This is why, as a first step, the traditional legal framework for information capture will be studied, leading to the need to create a specific law, as a second step.

18.1. The traditional legal framework for information capture

18.1.1. *Capture regulated by intellectual property law*

The author's rights, forming Book III of the intellectual property code, bring together all of the prerogatives of the author of an intellectual work, as well as his or her assignees (heirs and production companies).

This is made up of a moral dimension and a patrimonial dimension, which can be summarized in the following two tables:

---

3 Quessada, D., "De la sousveillance" ("On *Sousveillance*"), Multitudes 1/2010 (no. 40), pp. 54–59.
4 Bentham, J., *Panoptique : mémoire sur un nouveau principe pour construire des maisons d'inspection, et nommément des maisons de force* (*Panopticon, or the inspection house: containing the idea of a new principle of construction applicable to any sort of establishment, in which persons of any description are to be kept under inspection; and in particular to penitentiary-houses*), ed. Etienne Dumont, Paris, 1791; Mille et Une Nuits, Paris, 2002.
5 Ganascia, J.-G., *Voir et pouvoir: qui nous surveille ?* (*Surveillance and power: who is watching us?*) Paris, Ed. le Pommier, 2009.

Right of disclosure	The author has the power to decide the means and the time of the first contact of his or her work with the public.
Right of authorship	Any author must state unequivocally the name and occupation of the author of the work.
Right of integrity	The author can oppose any modification, distortion or desecration of his or her work and any infringement harmful to his or her reputation or good name.
Right to reconsider or withdraw	The author can withdraw a work which has already been disclosed in return for compensation for his or her assignee and the owners of the medium and the market.

Table 18.1. *Types of moral dimension of the author's rights as codified in the Intellectual Property Code*

This right is inalienable, almost always permanent, and imprescriptible.

Right of reproduction	The possibility to copy any or all parts of the work through its physical binding in a medium.
Right to representation	The right to communicate the work to the public.
Resale right	This allows visual arts authors to participate economically through the resale of their works.
Distribution right	This allows the author to decide on the location and the number of copies in the distribution of his or her work.

Table 18.2. *Types of patrimonial dimension of the author's rights as codified in the Intellectual Property Code*

18.1.2. *A legal context ill-suited to open science*

Given the typologies presented, it must be noted that the author's right seems unsuited to developing open science. In fact, the author's right seems to be the privilege of publishers, who form an influential political force, particularly through the French National Publishers Union (Syndicat National de l'Edition) which opposes most current data openness projects[6].

---

6 On this subject, see Malka, R., *La gratuité, c'est le vol. 2015 : la fin du droit d'auteur ?* (*Freedom is theft. 2015: the end of author's rights?*), Editions Richard, 2015.

As well as specific policies on business logic that they have put in place themselves, publishers will sometimes pay authors, including in the field of university presses, for free access to their publication[7]. This business logic, guided by an oligopolistic situation as large publishers such as Elsevier concentrate many of their resources[8], can cause harm to both science and its distribution. Is the author's right therefore an outdated right, ill-suited to the current openness in the field of science?

This question arises all the more given the increases in sharing platforms and networks, including APIs and user-generated content.

An API is commonly defined as a standardized set of categories, methods and functions which act as an interface through which a piece of software provides services to other software, each one being unique and having its own ways and means. They are presented within operating systems, systems for managing databases, programming languages or even application servers; among these, the two prime examples are Windows API[9] and Sockets[10].

User-generated content, for its part, is defined as all media with content mainly produced or directly influenced by end users. This emerged during the 2000s, marking the beginning of the Web 2.0 era and accompanying the appearance of new technologies.

Blogs, podcasts, the various Wikis and even Open Street Maps[11] are examples of this. The latter often use free or open source software, and are based on new copyright licenses, including Creative Commons, which are more flexible and facilitate collaboration between individuals who may be scattered over a wide geographic area.

Nonetheless, a problem arises: who owns the content created in this manner? The managers? The users? Furthermore, how can the production of such content be regulated or managed? This is not to mention the issue of plagiarism.

---

7 For an overview of the open access models in the humanities and social sciences, see http://www.openaccess-shs.info/wp-content/uploads/2015/10/Etude-IDATE-CAIRN-INFO-20151002.pdf.

8 http://www.cnrs.fr/dist/z-outils/documents/Distinfo2/Distinf14.pdf.

9 https://msdn.microsoft.com/fr-fr/library/windows/desktop/ff818516%28v=vs.85%29.aspx.

10 http://socket.io/docs/server-api/.

11 http://openstreetmap.fr/.

18.2. The clear need for a specific law

As well as these questions, which are sometimes the subject of difficulties as regards the ability of traditional law to resolve them, two basic thoughts emerge in current discussions: the legal certification of APIs and the creation of an open science law.

18.2.1. *What is the legal qualification of APIs?*

APIs, insofar as they constitute a relatively new tool, cause numerous problems with regard to their legal certification.

The latter is defined as an "intellectual operation which enables the application of the rule of law, by understanding the *de facto* elements through legal mechanisms, and the result of this intellectual operation".

This legal qualification has now become urgent, in light of the importance of APIs in economic models.

Furthermore, the Tech Trends 2015[12] study, published by the consultancy firm Deloitte, identifies the API economy as a major trend, with over 10,000 public APIs involving sectors as varied as social networks, e-commerce, telecommunications, connected objects, localization services, the transport sector (driverless cars) and even banks (banking APIs).

Consubstantially to the expansion of this economic model, since 2012 an even more topical legal debate has emerged, largely revolving around the question of whether or not APIs must pertain to an author's right rule.

There are three positions in this debate:

– European Court of Justice, May 2012[13]: the ECJ maintains that the features of a computer program and programming language cannot be protected by the author's right. The buyer of a program license therefore has the right to study or test its features in order to determine its basic principles.

12 http://www2.deloitte.com/global/en/pages/public-sector/articles/gx-public-sector-tech-trends-api-economy-report.html.
13 See http://www.alain-bensoussan.com/wp-content/uploads/2015/07/22684756.pdf.

– The United States Court of Appeals, 2014[14]: from which it has emerged that APIs constitute sufficiently structured and established (individualized) works of language to be eligible for protection under the rights of the author.

– Lemaire draft law[15], 2015. This anticipates, at the time of consultation, "offering citizens Application Programming Interfaces (API) which are technically secure and governed by a stable right shared at the European level" and "developing to this end an 'EU connect' label for these APIs, enabling them to be certified in accordance with public and private users"[16].

18.2.2. *Moving toward the creation of an open science law?*

Despite the development having exceeded all known speed limits in digital technology in the world of "platforms", it should be noted that there are no specific regulations as they remain reliant on trade law.

Science in France is thus currently subject to intellectual property law: the platforms control all data, including its reuse. However, as we have said, the author's right seem to be bound by the development of scientific research and the distribution of knowledge; this is the origin of the idea shared by different actors involved in the discussion on establishing open science as a "universal principle" and a "natural law" in order to avoid trade regulating the use of digital platforms by consolidating data and research results.

By establishing such a law, it therefore becomes a matter of counteracting commercial logic on knowledge distribution, on the one hand, in order to align it with existing economic models (in the United States and Germany, for example), which would lead, on the other hand, to leaving behind the logical incongruity of a scientific field subject to a law and a model developed largely by literary creations.

Given that the Internet is a *chiaroscuro* world where there is no space for Manichaeism, it is essential to have understated temperance in a balance between producing, maintaining and publishing resources.

---

14 See http://www.alain-bensoussan.com/wp-content/uploads/2014/05/28131372.pdf.
15 https://www.republique-numerique.fr/.
16 See   http://www.republique-numerique.fr/projects/projet-de-loi-numerique/consultation/consultation/opinions/section-3-loyaute-des-plateformes/normalisation-des-application-programming-interfaces-api-interfaces-de-programmation.

Indeed, the new information and communication technologies, the Internet and so on, intrinsically have an almost Utopian dimension of democratization, as well as the promise of its extreme opposite with, for example, sousveillance phenomena, the ultimate Orwellian theme.

A possible alternative which would enable us to avoid a double pitfall of a utopian democracy in the digital arena making knowledge freely accessible on the one hand and a society subject to the dangers of sousveillance or improper capturing on the other hand would be a law on open science inscribed in legislation as a fundamental right.

19

Public Knowledge Policies in the Digital Age

According to the French Council of State (Conseil d'Etat), a digital platform is a site which "allows third parties to suggest content, services and goods or which provides access to such content, application stores, content-sharing services, marketplaces …"[1].

They are often described as being at the heart of a two-sided market, the interface between consumers and businesses, and as having specific exchanges with the two actors. The best-known platforms are the GAFA companies – Google, Apple, Facebook and Amazon. Financial platforms, the product of technological innovations and intended to improve the productivity of the sector, are often presented as the archetypal digital platforms.

Just like financial platforms, digital platforms are a source of innovation and development as much for consumers as for producers, as they offer fast and easy access to resources and international markets. The development of these platforms is exponential and global, making regulations complicated to implement.

1 See Chaire Innovation & Régulation des Services Numériques, *Compte rendu de la conférence – La Régulation des Plateformes Numériques.* 07/04/2015. P 2. http:// innovation-regulation2. telecom-paristech.fr/wp-content/uploads/2015/06/La-R%C3%A9gulation-des-Plateformes-Num% C3%A9riques-CR-Defdef.pdf.

Founded on openness to all and constant innovation, the current system, or the economic model for digital platforms, has led to the creation of monopolies within the sector, separating their ecosystems to maintain their position of dominance. Two instruments are used to combat these trends: competition and the right of the community.

It is necessary to regulate digital platforms as various trends have been observed in the digital platform sector.

19.1. GAFA domination and the oligopolization of the market

The economic model of digital platforms has led to the creation of monopolies in the sector. The domination of the GAFA companies is indisputable.

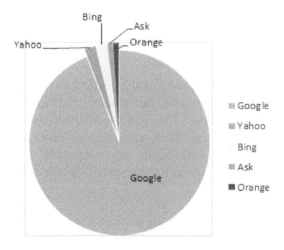

Figure 19.1. *The most used search engines in the world (2014)*

Today, the maxim that the winner takes all dominates the platforms sector. For instance, initially, Facebook was in competition with Myspace. Offering, according to users, a better service than Myspace, Facebook won over the market and today has over a billion users. The same occurred with Google and its operating system which has long been competing but which is currently installed on over 80% of the world's smartphones. The same could be noted again for Microsoft with computers. The competition, strong to begin with, no longer exists once the dominant position has been taken.

A monopoly only poses a problem if no other actor can challenge this domination. The current system for digital platforms does not allow monopolies to be challenged. The economic model for platforms at once rests on the free provision of services to consumers, in return for collecting their personal data and content, and on the enhancement of this data, including by offering visibility to producers.

The better the service provided by a platform, the more visitors it has, and the greater the visibility it provides. In a system where the dominant player occupies the entire market, a new actor cannot take its place as there are no more data to be collected and enhanced.

As a result, it is difficult to believe that the current monopolies can be dethroned, even with the emergence of new giants, the NATU companies – Netflix, Airbnb, Tesla and Uber.

However, they do not challenge the existence of the GAFA companies. A monopoly is legitimate when it draws its revenue from a return on investment and not from independent means unconnected to this information, such as an informational annuity. Monopolies are especially problematic as the market is no longer two-sided but three-sided due to the network effect. The innovations brought by start-ups must pass through monopolistic platforms to become known.

This dependence is particularly strong as the GAFA companies often purchase and adapt applications. Numerous start-ups have become subsidiaries of the GAFA companies; YouTube was bought by Google and Instagram by Facebook.

The digital platform system, by enhancing and capturing the data of Internet users through a number of platforms, has led to the creation of monopolies which are difficult to challenge.

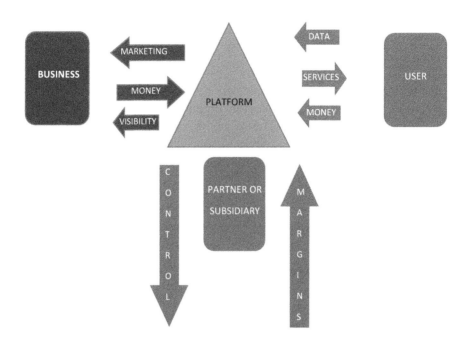

Figure 19.2. *Digital platforms are central to three economic relationships*[2]

19.2. Isolated digital ecosystems

The success of these platforms is due to the performance of the services offered. They know how to create a digital ecosystem suited to the needs of Internet users. Initially open to everyone, these ecosystems have closed in order to maximize and maintain existing monopolies.

One of the innovations brought about by these platforms is the customization of the Internet for Internet users, as well as the fact that the Internet user is not aware of this customization. As a result, the user is unaware that the content proposed, initially, was selected from several relevant results.

---

2 Conseil National du Numérique (National Council of Digital Technology), report on the neutrality of platforms. 21 September 2015. http://www.cnnumerique.fr/wp-content/uploads/2014/06/CNNum_Rapport_Neutralite_des_plateformes.pdf [consulted 25 September 2015].

When an Internet user uses the search engine Google, the results displayed correspond to his or her preferences and not to an exhaustive list of relevant results. Due to Adwords, Google transforms the list of results into an advertising insert without informing the user.

To preserve their monopoly, digital platforms have also made different actors dependent on their services, isolating their digital ecosystem. For any one service, there are several versions according to the ecosystem. Google and Apple offer their own email applications, for example. They offer their own services for buying music, applications, instant messaging, operating systems and so on.

Depending on the service, the user is often not free to move between the ecosystems. It is not possible to use the Appstore on an Android smartphone, for example. To make their new services known, they also use the cross-network effect, i.e. the exchange of data between platforms belonging to an identical group. Your data collected on YouTube are used by the Google Shopping platform. In this way, it is dependent on one of the dominant platforms.

The platforms deny the interoperability of their service with others. There is also an obstacle to the portability of content between platforms. It is difficult to transfer a list of Facebook contacts to another platform, for instance. While entering a platform is free, leaving it comes at a cost for the Internet user.

The economic model of digital platforms, centered on enhancing the data of Internet users, has encouraged the emergence of monopolies. In order to maintain their status and maximize their profits, the monopolistic platforms have developed their service provision, to the detriment of users and the openness of their digital ecosystem.

Regulators must take action against the oligopolization of the digital platform sector, which is happening at the expense of users.

19.3. Regulation through competition law

In the digital platform sector, the main instrument used in regulation is competition.

In a sector where innovation is at the heart of the system, competition creates innovation. The most innovative platform replaces the old ones. Traditional players in the economy sometimes turn up to compete with new ones by uniting to create their platform, such as the hotels and restaurants in Nantes with fairbooking.com to counter large platforms such as booking.com.

This competition is, however, distorted by the winner takes all principle and its long-term consequences. The comparison between digital and financial platforms is relevant here. Once a platform has taken the dominant position, no innovation can survive without it and it appropriates the innovation, as we have seen with Google and YouTube.

Competition law intervenes to guarantee competition. The competition authority sets itself several tasks within the regulation of digital platforms: keeping the playing field open and competitive, promoting alternatives and European preferences, reducing dependence on platforms and combating the effects of exclusion.

Article L. 420-2 of the commercial code guarantees this competition by prohibiting abuse of dominance by stipulating that an actor's practices are forbidden if they "aim or are able, as a result, to prevent, restrict or distort the competition in a market".

At the beginning of 2015, the European Commission accused Google of abusing its dominant position. The same proceedings had been launched by Microsoft in 2009. At the start of 2016, the FTC (Federal Trade Commission) launched an inquiry into the abuse of its dominant position by Google and its Android system in the United States.

Even if there will always be innovation and competition, at least on a small scale, in the platforms market, current competition law seems powerless to tackle the hegemony of the GAFA companies in the sector.

19.4. Data protection: moving toward a law for the digital community

The best way to counter these monopolistic trends is by protecting personal data, which can only be effective by recognizing the laws protecting the community of users of these platforms.

Edouard Geffray, secretary general of the National Commission for Information Technology and Freedoms (Commission Nationale de l'Informatique et des Libertés (CNIL)), maintains that "personal data is the elementary particle of digital technology"[3]. The GAFA companies have built their monopoly through their innovations but preserve it due to the data they have, making it vital for all other actors in the sector.

While the data will be available to some actors, the competition between actors will not be effective. In a digital world where all data – personal, content or metadata – will be available to everyone, to the extent that it can be considered common property, competition will be effective as there will be no informational income and there will be no dependence on the GAFA companies.

However, this option poses a problem with regard to personal data. It has been given by Internet users to one or another platform in return for being able to use the platform and not to be distributed publicly.

The CNIL is the body for monitoring the collection of personal data, while the ARCEP (Regulatory Authority for Electronic Communications and Postal Services – Autorité de Régulation de Communications Electronique et des Postes) intervenes more widely in regulating the field of digital technology.

The CNIL recently condemned Google for their illicit collection of personal data and imposed a 150,000 Euro fine on the company. In 2014, the European Commission published a ruling aimed at limiting the unfair terms on data collection in platform usage contracts. Article 113-3 of the consumer code also obliges digital platforms to show transparency and loyalty to consumers. Internet users must be aware of the use of their data by platforms. The search engine Google is supposed to inform its users that it showcases sites belonging to the Google group, currently known as Alphabet, or which have paid to be among the first results.

---

3 See Chair of Innovation and Regulation of Digital Services, *Report of the Conference – The Regulation of Digital Platforms) Compte rendu de la conférence – La Régulation des Plateformes Numériques.* 7 April 2015. P 33. http://innovation-regulation2.telecom-paristech.fr/wp-content/uploads/2015/06/La-R%C3%A9gulation-des-Plateformes-Num%C3%A9riques-CR-Def def.pdf.

The current regulations do not seem to respond fully to the problems posed by digital platforms. Laws on competition, trade, consumers and data protection are being developed to dismantle the monopolies and make the operation of platforms less opaque.

However, the current regulations do not meet to the challenges of interoperability and compatibility between platforms. These regulations are undergoing enormous change, just like digital platforms themselves. They are adapting by promoting the protection of data and their use, thereby making the largest possible amount of data accessible. This is also occurring at the European and international levels. State regulations seem to coincide on these topics.

The Politics of Creating Artificial Intelligence

Artificial intelligence (AI) can be defined as the set of theories and techniques implemented to make machines capable of simulating human intelligence.

Two categories of AI must be taken into consideration. On the one hand, so-called "strong" AI which should be able to produce intelligent behavior, and experience real self-awareness, feelings and an understanding of its reasoning. This AI is predicted to appear by 2050 and would be the result of a development bringing the intelligence of machines closer to that of human beings.

On the other hand, so-called "weak" AI aims to build independent systems with algorithms capable of resolving technical problems by simulating intelligence. Less sophisticated than "strong" AI, "weak" AI is already available today. It can be found, for example, in connection with robots, such as in the Google Car, a vehicle capable of driving independently in accordance with its environment due to sensors and geolocalization.

It was Alan Turing who laid the foundations for AI in 1950 in his famous work "Computing Machinery and Intelligence", by imagining a test intended to simulate human psychology in such a way that a person conversing with a teleprinter, ignorant of it being a machine, would be fooled by it.

The concept of AI, far from being new, is thus already over 60 years old and concerns numerous sectors with applications as diverse as they are innovative as far as independent objects are concerned, in e-commerce, smart content, health, finance and so on.

More generally, we can also ponder the purposes of this separation. Transhumanism seems to be one of the aims behind the development of AI. This ideology, which emerged in the 1950s, aims to increase human capabilities – physical and mental – by making use of all available scientific and technological means. If this ideology were pursued in the future, the decline of death would be unavoidable.

According to Laurent Alexandre, a company like Google could participate in this process by mastering the technologies necessary to achieving it: robotics, computing, search engines and AI, nano- and biotechnologies, and DNA sequencing, the cost of which "has fallen by three million in ten years"[1].

20.1. History

20.1.1. *From joy to "the winter of artificial intelligence"*

In the aftermath of the World War II, scientists were convinced that the creation of an AI was possible and that it would happen soon, while also considering it essential to carrying out tasks with abilities equal or superior to human abilities. American universities in particular, such as Harvard, Stanford and even MIT with its MAC – Mathematics and Computer – project from 1963, have been involved in this project, supported by the DARPA, the research branch of the US Army, which has injected millions of dollars into different research groups in this way.

Numerous fields of research are thereby explored, such as connectionism which bases AI on a neuron network, the General Problem Solver based on the analysis of aims and means and the construction of semantic networks, where the meaning of words only appear for machines in connection to other words.

---

1 http://pasfaux.com/le-cout-du-sequencage.

Despite this enthusiasm and these, significant but vague, efforts, disillusionment began to take hold in around 1975, as computers remained primitive in relation to the initial objectives. One of the main reasons of this failure concerns the underestimation of the enormous capabilities provided by the human brain. The latter was in fact the starting point and the reference point for research under way in AI, but it has continued to be seen as a simple mechanism, which it manifestly is not.

20.1.2. *A recurrent failure*

The revival of research in AI took place in the 1980s, principally in Japan where the MITI (the Ministry of International Trade and Industry), invested almost a billion dollars to design more powerful computers so that, as Turing wished, they would be able to talk like humans and interpret images presented to them. Nonetheless, even there, failure endured.

These ambitions have, at worst, been abandoned, and at best been scaled down. At MIT, they are restricting themselves to primitive intelligence, as shown in insects. Robots in insect form have been designed, benefiting from the miniaturization of components during the technical progress of the 1980s.

20.1.3. *The "spring of artificial intelligence" rediscovered*

The 2000s provided happier results, enabled in part by strong growth in the power of computers in connection with Moore's law, which predicted that computer power would experience an exponential growth and double every year.

The other factor behind the acceleration we have seen for several years in the design of AI can be explained largely by the birth of big data: the collection, storage and processing of large amounts of data.

It is the union of these two factors, largely due to technical progress, which explains the current development. We must note here that the majority of algorithms which now allow AI to function were written years before; the only innovation has therefore been incremental through the new technical means available.

The application of both old research and more recent discoveries has therefore allowed large firms, such as Google, to develop the "deep learning" technique. It concerns functioning in stages, and consists of presenting a computer with millions of images representing a single object or living being so that it can discover a concept by itself.

In this case, Google managed to introduce the concept of a cat to its Google Brain software in 2012, through the three-day analysis of 10 million screen captures from YouTube[2].

20.2. Artificial intelligence has become a priority for public and private actors

20.2.1. *Mass investment from the private sector*

The private sector currently invests massively in the field of AI. In this regard, on 2 June 2015, Facebook opened an AI research center in Paris went on to have 40–50 researchers.

This interest also translates into purchasing businesses; Google acquired Boston Dynamics, which works with the US Department of Defense, and the British company Deepmind, another business working with the "deep learning" technique, for 500 million dollars.

20.2.2. *Smart content*

We use "weak" AI on a daily basis. Google, the big name in the sector, is thus in the process of launching Inbox, a new and more structured version of Gmail which allows better classification of emails through an intelligent algorithm which analyses the behavior of users.

On the other hand, data which come into our messaging inboxes also serve to identify our preferences in order to suggest the most targeted

---

2 https://www.youtube.com/watch?v=MRG8eq7miUE.

advertising possible, in response to our immediate or future expectations. It is this "intelligent" management of content we can access or which is suggested to us on communications interfaces that is known as "smart content".

Success is achievable. Google took in 50 billion dollars in advertising revenue in 2014 through this technique, gathered through its search engine as much as through free and efficient services such as Gmail and Inbox. Facebook's revenue rests on the same logic, and Amazon also uses these intelligent algorithms to suggest tempting products to its clients.

However, this practice does raise the issue of personal data usage, and more specifically of privacy. Indeed, with the lack of any option enabling access to personal data, including analysis of mail received, to be prohibited, user protection appears to be reduced, and the partiality of Google can also specifically be called into question.

This issue is even more pressing for businesses where data confidentiality and secrecy prove to be crucial.

20.2.3. *Public actors are aware of the importance of artificial intelligence*

In France, the Institute for Intelligent Systems and Robotics (*Institut des Systèmes Intelligents et de Robotique* (ISIR)) brings together researchers in the fields of computing and AI, and neurosciences in particular. The interest of this Institute is in promoting synergies between biology and the engineering sciences.

At the European level, the ambitious "brain project", launched by the European Commission, aims to simulate the human brain through a supercomputer by around 2024. There is in this regard, at long last, noticeable international cooperation, such as that led by the National Institute for Research in Computer and Control Sciences (*Institut National de la Recherche en Informatique et Automatique* (INRIA)) within the framework of the ESPRIT project for research and development in information technology.

While cooperation between developed States is frequent, the defining feature of this project lies in the connection between French research teams and those from emerging countries, in this case Brazil.

Public authorities thereby also engage in researching AI, at different levels including national and European, or through international cooperation which allows knowledge relevant to the field to be shared.

20.4. The appearance of legal problems

AI has numerous applications and armies are already aware of this. The United States is therefore testing the "Big Dog"[3], a four-legged robot capable of acting quickly and accurately when faced with complicated situations, and which currently transports materials.

At the same time, other armies that have more lethal potential and are in possession of AI are experienced, such as with machine guns or missile launch systems.

The use of this standalone military equipment raises the issues of respect for the body of international humanitarian law and wars fought by robots. While the 1977 additional protocol to the Geneva Conventions requires States to "assess the legality of new weapons", Human Rights Watch, in the report it published in April 2015, highlights the difficulty of determining responsibilities in cases of crime.

The report thereby notes that "the mechanisms of legal responsibility are unsuitable and insufficient for responding to illegal damages which could bring about entirely autonomous systems".

Indeed, who would be prosecuted in an infraction of international law? The company that made the machine, the one that developed the algorithms, the authority or soldier using the weapons? The issue of distinguishing between civilians and combatants is central to these questions.

AI offers tremendous possibilities for human development in highly varied sectors. Nonetheless, it is also proving to be necessary to restrict the

---

3 https://www.youtube.com/watch?v=TA4ARPs0R-E.

development of its usage. As underlined by the attorney Alain Bensoussan, the lack of a law supervising the use of robots with AI, at both the national and international levels, is glaring. At best, it would guide the development of the new technologies which are, already, establishing themselves in our lives.

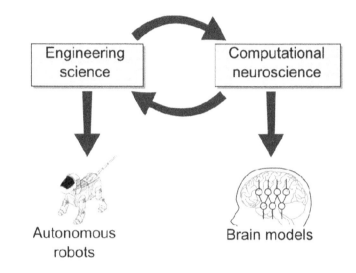

Figure 20.1. *Link between human intelligence and artificial intelligence*

Security Policies in Artificial Intelligence

After having presented the different dimensions of Artificial Intelligence (AI), a second stage, on how to secure this intelligence, is taking shape.

AI is an important developing field of science which brings with it major technological innovations. While in recent years AI has improved largely due to the sensors that have been developed, it is expected that future research will succeed in significantly improving the actual intelligence of machines. Such advances will need to be accompanied by deep ethical, political and legal reflections on AI.

Making AI secure requires a double ethical and practical reflection. Ethical because it is necessary to define the framework and the field of what rights we would grant to machines in the future; practical because it is equally important to decide what applications we would take from AI, namely, which innovations we would allow to develop in the economy. These two questions are the two key pillars which must guide thoughts on the security of AI.

Speaking of security as both ethical and practical still implies a need for the clear definition of what is to be secured. AI is based on intelligent data processing, and therefore a kind of information processing which is able to adapt and memorize information. Intelligent data processing can be divided into two main groups.

On the one hand, this allows AI to create dual digital technologies: we leave traces on the Internet and our digital footprint is increasingly coming to resemble who we really are. What is to be done with this split digital personality? Must we authorize it? How can it be controlled?

On the other hand, data processing also allows AI to make decisions, which can affect a multitude of events in our daily lives. If a robot with AI is capable of making a decision, what legal status should it have? How can this decision-making be supervised?

21.1. Security as a comment on machines and data

21.1.1. *Freedom for machines?*

The first step to securing AI is taking the decision on the use of data utilized by machines. This new use of data can be considered overall by splitting the whole in two[1].

We do in fact increasingly delegate our data to machines, computers and AI which are already partially capable of processing these data. There is therefore a kind of consensual and controlled transfer of personal information, and the challenge lies in thinking ahead to when this process can take place.

It entails a kind of practical relationship between a robot with AI and humanity, as well as reflection on the consequences for making these data sharing secure. Eric Sadin, for instance, talks about a future where we will be "organic-digital" terminals: we will be surrounded by waves and data. One of the challenges of making AI secure consists of arbitration between filtration and a reinforcement of these data in order to make proposals.

In fact, this new relationship between robots and humans is leading to a new kind of exchange, in which it is possible to envisage owning a personal robot, an assistant[2] which would be responsible for improving our lives through its superhuman capacity to manage data.

---

1 Eric Sadin, *La société de l'anticipation* (*The Science Fiction Society*), 2011. Editions Inculte, Paris.
2 See above.

These data could concern, among other things, our health (physical parameters), our use of time or our tastes and could be a set of data which robots would use to take micro-decisions for us; making or moving an appointment, suggesting a meal suited to our mood and body type and so on. The data could also be continuously exchanged for others within the robot for these microdecisions in cloud computing. In other words, AI would enable us to form digital images of ourselves which would serve to improve or regulate our daily lives.

The example chosen here does not, of course, represent all of the potential applications of AI. It is simply an effective way of envisaging the new relationship that could exist between AI and humankind, through this new data processing. The challenge of security at this individual level consists of a clear demarcation of the field of action and interventions left to different kinds of AI in daily life.

In pursuing our practical reflections on the use of data by AI, we must also think about the economic aspect of this new relationship, which we will go on to describe. The logical progression of data use is its commercialization. A personal robot could transform the economy (and is already on the way to doing so) through a completely different relationship with consumption. The major change, in fact, would be the transformation with regard to time. If robots come to permanently exchange data on us and our lives, it is possible that we will have an uninterrupted personalized relationship.

This relationship would be individualized as each robot with AI would store a sufficiently large amount of data to be able to estimate that these data could define us as we really are. The relationship would also be continuous as this exchange of data by robots, through a cloud, for instance, would continuously and simultaneously adapt to our behavior. The robot would know about our heartbeat, our tiredness, any changes in our use of time and so on.

For a futuristic moment, this situation could seem to resemble a form of capitalism where the concept of time is transformed by ceasing to exist. A continuous individualized relationship, in this case, would be a means through which we would no longer have to concern ourselves with small purchases to be made, and we would therefore leave a certain number of decisions to AI systems. There is a breakdown here between the desire to make a purchase and the data used instantaneously for a commercialization that enables instant exchange.

21.1.2. How far should we go?

The example developed up to this point allows us to take advantage of the first level of security with which we will be confronted. This choice should be made at an individual level: we must decide how much data we wish to entrust to AIs and which uses these AI will make of it.

Security is in fact not only expressed in law in terms of responsibility. The first step is for practical reflection on the use of AI, the problems of which have been illustrated by the example here. This first stage can be considered to be security, insofar as it will restrict the framework into which legal standards enabling AI itself to be made secure will be integrated.

The first stage is therefore similar to a reflective process which could take the form of a national civic debate with the participation of all civil society, inter alia citizens, the State, scientists and organizations. The red arrows in the following diagram correspond to the next stages of regulation.

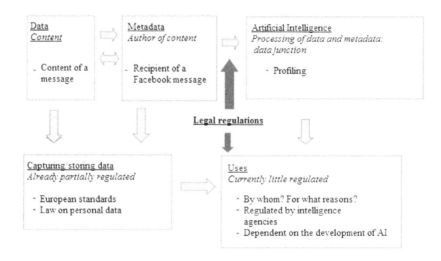

Figure 21.1. *Legal Process for data and artificial intelligence*

21.2. From the security of machines to the security of humans

In the first section, we treated AI as if it had a real status. However, the law does not address relationships between humans and machines, but rather only between humans. It is therefore necessary to question the management of the new uses of data that will come to affect us.

One of the major challenges of this second stage of security is decision-making. It is necessary to decide how far to delegate and determine the manner in which the law will grasp this issue.

Before taking this reflection further, the term "data mining" must be explained correctly. According to a document from the United States General Accounting Office, data mining consists of applying "database technology and techniques (such as statistical analysis and modeling) to uncover hidden patterns and subtle relationships in data and to infer rules that allow for the prediction of future results".

In order to better understand this data connection, we can quote Saint Thomas Aquinas, whose words were able to explain, some centuries in advance, what data mining represents:

> "However this mysterious presentiment of the future is produced, it is impossible to see what it is. Yet it is already neither past nor future but present. When we state that we can see the future, what we see are not events themselves, which do not yet exist, that is to say they are in the future, but rather their causes or perhaps the signs that foreshadow them and which already exist: they are not of the future, but of the present to clairvoyants and it is thanks to them that the future is conceived by the soul and foretold. These notions already exist, and predicting the future is to see what is already present."

Predicting the future is in fact analyzing data and facts and is limited in the case of human intelligence as we can only analyze and manage a limited amount of data and information. Extremely powerful computers can already separate and analyze infinitely larger amounts of data than we are able to process. However, we are not yet at the stage where the forms of

AI can make decisions, primarily because AIs do not have their own memories. We will not go into the technical details of AI here so that we may concentrate on the process of making potential decision-making secure.

21.2.1. *Can machines be made responsible?*

The fate of this decision lies with data mining, and would allow robots of other AI containers to take more or less important decisions. The first problem in such decision-making, other than the fact that a human is not necessarily involved in the decisions, is the performative power of such predictions.

In other words, the fact that robots foreshadow a tendency toward human decision-making which follows and is able to participate if certain events actually occur. The simple act of making this prediction could cause the action itself.

To illustrate this, we can take the film Minority Report as an example. In this film, a machine predicts crimes to be committed in the future, which allows police officers to prevent them. Yet, at one point, the machine predicts an event which would not have happened had it not made the prediction, and it therefore makes a mistake. Here, we are able to understand the initial limit to this AI decision-making, and which could not easily be surpassed.

How is this issue currently addressed in law? Given that, at present, such decision-making is impossible, there are not really any specific laws on robots or AI. We must therefore look to the 1978 French Data Protection Act to find the existing legal framework.

Predictably, at the time it was written, this law could not predict the development of AI and yet the text of articles 2 and 3 anticipate that "a human decision-maker must break the automatic linkage of reasoning to evaluate, or even correct, the outcome in accordance with subjective and circumstantial elements". A type of AI able to make decisions is therefore already regulated to some extent.

21.2.2. *Data and metadata: where should machines stop?*

Besides the issue of decision-making, the status of data which has been created in this way raises another legal issue relating to making the AI secure. Up to this point, we have addressed the philosophical question of the responsibility a machine can bear in making a decision. However, the information that this decision is based on is in fact metadata arising from connection to personal data.

Personal data in computing were actually defined in the 1978 Data Protection Act, which also regulates its use. These data can relate to all of our information, inter alia, name, date of birth, blood group and Internet footprint.

These personal data therefore have a clear and regulated status. However, the relevant part in cases of AI is in fact a collection of these data which form metadata, and yet metadata does not currently have a clear status.

We will therefore return to the topic of the virtual person, which we touched on earlier. Through personal data, AIs can in fact create a virtual identity, which is moving increasingly close to that of a real person. The moment when these two identities are so alike that they could practically merge together poses numerous problems for the law, which does not yet provide for such a case. Nonetheless, the Data Protection Act is the primary (not to say the only) framework for this issue.

At present, it is article 10 of the act which could be a barrier to use of metadata (which is the foundation of a virtual person supposed to represent us). The law in fact states that "no legal ruling involving an assessment of a person's behavior can be the basis for the automated processing of personal data intended to evaluate certain aspects of his or her personality".

In other words, a legal ruling cannot currently be based on a comparison of data by any kind of AI, whatever it may be. By expecting a legal body to be created for the metadata which can form a virtual person, the law therefore prohibits the justice system using such data.

However, it is clear that such a response is unsatisfactory. If the aim is to make AI secure, it is necessary to think how we would like to see this kind of data supervised and legislated. This is an essential part of our thought process. At present, the individual and his or her profile are two distinct entities, although the virtual profile currently has no status in such cases. It is, however, too early to define this status; we can in fact consider that for now such a profile has neither the detail nor the reliability required to be considered a legal entity in its own right. Although as we have said, we will not resolve this debate here in order to concentrate solely on cases where a connection between profile and person would or should be made. Given the current ambiguity surrounding the law on these data, it would be useful to replace a virtual person, for instance, which would be based on the model of a legal fiction.

As a legal person, this virtual person "would have the legal rights and obligations which would be attributed following a catalogue of resources that we would discuss in a virtual community and with regard to the rules governing this community"[3]. The thought process should be taken as accompanied by an equally important reflection on the place we wish to grant usage, which could be carried out by this entity, going forward.

Finally, the status of robots that include AI must be considered. Indeed, if such machines make decisions, they are responsible, just like the creator of the algorithm, the machine's manufacturer and finally, potentially, the machine itself.

In this way, this latter responsibility would correspond to the creation of a robot law, which would be based on Asimov's three laws[4]. Such thoughts have begun to be considered by several leading legal figures.

---

3 Danièle Bourcier, "De l'intelligence artificielle à la personne virtuelle : émergence d'une entité juridique ?" ("From artificial intelligence to the virtual person: the emergence of a legal entity?"), *Droit et société* 2001/3 (no. 49), (online).

4 We are thinking here of three laws written by the famous novelist: (1) a robot may not injure a human being or, through inaction, allow a human being to come to harm, (2) a robot must obey the orders given it by human beings except where such orders would conflict with the first law, (3) a robot must protect its own existence as long as such protection does not conflict with the first or second laws. We can also add the zero law: a robot may not harm humanity, or, by inaction, allow humanity to come to harm.

This last stage in making AI secure is not the most urgent, although nowadays it is possible that we could have need of such a law, which would fill the gaps that current laws could leave.

Conclusion

It is difficult to conclude. All of the changes described here are still underway and as yet have no permanent conclusions. Our work, while modest, seems at least able to give us the means to keep up with the numerous debates mentioned within and, concerning us more directly, to facilitate in-depth studies on its foundations, preparing for other reflections and positions to be taken in the future...

Postscript – Perspectives on the Law Relating to a Digital Republic

When we began writing this work, the French digital legislation was still in draft form. It has taken us some months to write this work, which now allows us to provide a new perspective upon this legislation, which will update knowledge production issues.

The French National Assembly has ratified the text of the legislation which was put before it in June 2016. This is now in the process of being passed by parliament, after ratification by the Senate. The Bill, which is made up of 48 articles, has as its slogan *Freedom to innovate, Equality of laws, Fraternity of a form of digital accessible to all and the Exemplary nature of a modernizing state.* It addresses subjects as varied as Net neutrality (equal treatment for users, in terms of quality of connections), portability of data (the obligation, for Internet Service Providers (ISPs) to organize the transfer of user data), maintaining Internet connections (by implementing a so-called "solidarity fund" for the poorest households), the confidentiality of private exchanges, the right to privacy of minors allowing them (or indeed their parents or guardians) to request that data, photos or texts be deleted, but also the issues of public open data, the end of digital and e-sports. The text, which was subject to public consultation in September 2015, received 8,000 citizen contributions.

This work has explained the changes which digital has imposed upon the production, dissemination and the increase in the value of knowledge production. These changes should thus be understood by public authorities, to protect citizens from the potential abuses that they might cause (these include the use of data and the impact of web dissemination) but also with a view to exploiting the immense field of possibilities which they open up. This legislation unlocks solutions for France. The text may indeed become a European inspiration, in particular for the three points which directly affect knowledge production.

– *Data*

Open data allows scientific value to be produced. Article 9 will allow for both verification and research transparency. Raw data and the sharing of the same will enrich all approaches.

– *Publication*

Under the legislation, the relationship between the scientific author and publisher is rebalanced, particularly by means of Article 17. The author may, at the expiration of a time limit of between 6 to 12 months, publish his article freely, thus reducing the time period between his own self-publishing and that of the original publication of the work by the publisher. These thus amount to modified publication embargoes.

– *Text and data mining*

The exclusivity of research rights, processing, and searches for articles and documents which a publisher owns are deleted, although the financing of this research is 50% secured by public funding.

This law moves away from the themes, which have previously been tackled, of the commons or the laws relating to robots, but the latter remain in the preparation stage to be dealt with in future legislation. The law itself becomes an essential building block in the construction of a genuine temple of knowledge; this is a temple which is accessible to all and which shares all data. In this regard, we may resume, by translating the Latin motto of the Collège de France in Paris[1] *docet omnes omnia* as "Teach everyone everything."

Renaud FABRE, Quentin MESSERSCHMIDT-MARIET,
Margot HOLVOET
Paris,
September 2016

---

[1] This is a renowned teaching and research establishment specializing in sciences and humanities.

Glossary

Algorithm: An algorithm is "the study of resolving problems through the implementation of a succession of basic operations according to a defined process in order to reach a solution"[1]. An algorithm can also be considered a method or process enabling a particular problem to be resolved, and which is at the foundation of implementing a computer program, without taking a specific form[2].

Article processing charge (APC): The publication costs relating to the amount of money requested by publishers from the authors of scientific articles so that these articles are freely accessible to readers. Two kinds of periodical are involved: those where the articles are freely accessible in their entirety and those where a part of the articles is freely accessible (hybrid model)[3].

Artificial intelligence: The capability of a functional unit to carry out functions generally associated with human intelligence, such as reasoning and learning[4].

---

1 Arr. 27 June 1989, on improving the vocabulary of computer science, App., Shared provisions.
2 Hervé Wolff, "Le droit d'auteur protège-t-il les algorithmes ?" ("Does the author's right protect algorithms?"), Luxlegal Wordpress, 2011.
3 INIST glossary.
4 ISO Standard 2382-28.

Author–payer: "We refer to the author–payer model when the author or his or her affiliated institution or financial backer makes a contribution to the publisher to make the article freely accessible to all readers at no cost. This is in opposition to reader–payer and sponsor–payer models"[5].

Creative Commons: Creative Commons licenses aim to define the conditions of reuse and/or distribution of works, and, more specifically, of multimedia works distributed on the Internet. It involves providing a legal tool which at once guarantees the protection of the author's rights on his or her work and the circulation of the content of this work. Creative Commons licenses allow the public to be informed in advance of the author's decision to authorize certain uses of his or her work under certain conditions.

Crowdsourcing: The participation of amateurs who contribute to the development of real databases by compiling various kinds of information (photographs, specimen locations, etc.) and by providing knowledge of a primarily non-scientific nature.

Gold road: The gold road applies to the publication of articles in open access periodicals, regardless of their mode of financing. It corresponds to the second strategy recommended in the Budapest Open Access Initiative: "Alternative periodicals: secondly, scholars need means to launch a new generation of alternative periodicals engaged in open access and to assist existing periodicals that choose to make the transition to open access"[6].

Green road: The green road relates to self-archiving by researchers or archiving by a third party of articles in open archives. It corresponds to the first strategy recommended in the Budapest Open Access Initiative: "Self-archiving: firstly, scholars need instruments and assistance to deposit their articles with peer-reviewed journals in electronic open archives, a practice commonly known as self-archiving"[7].

Scientific and technical information (STI): "Scientific and technical information brings together all information produced in research and which

---

5 http://openaccess.inist.fr/spip.php?page=glossaire.
6 INIST glossary.
7 INIST glossary.

is necessary to both scientific activity and industry. By its very nature, scientific and technical information covers all scientific and technical sectors and comes in multiple forms: articles, scientific periodicals and works, technical specifications describing the manufacturing process, technical documentation that comes with products, patent notices, bibliographic databases, gray literature, banks of raw data, open archives and data repositories accessible on the Internet, portals, etc. ..."[8].

Lost science: All digital scientific publications that do not follow the traditional model of online release and use low key or little-known distribution channels.

Metadata: "Metadata is all structured data describing physical or digital resources. It is an essential link in information sharing and the interoperability of electronic resources. It is traditionally divided into descriptive, administrative and structural metadata"[9].

Open access: "The free and public provision of knowledge on the Internet, allowing everyone to read, download, copy, pass on, print, search or link to the complete text of articles, dissect them to index them, make use of it for software or for any other legal purpose, with no financial, legal or technical barriers other than those inseparable from access and Internet use"[10].

Open archive: The term "open archive" indicates a bank where data from scientific research and education are deposited and where access was open, i.e. barrier-free. This openness is made possible through the use of common protocols that facilitate the accessibility of content from several repositories maintained by different data providers[11].

Open data: This refers to the data that a body makes universally available as digital files in order to enable its reuse. Open data are not generally personal

---

8 http://www.enseignementsup-recherche.gouv.fr/cid20438/les-missions-de-l-information-scientifique-et-technique.html.
9 INIST glossary.
10 INIST glossary.
11 INIST glossary.

and are accessible in a format encouraging its reuse. The reuse of open data can be subject to conditions[12].

Open process: The right to proceed freely to the observation of data through the use of digital tools for processing, analysis or exploration.

Open science: This refers to permanent and free Internet access to data from scientific research and education, as well as the right to proceed freely to the observation of these data through digital tools for processing, analysis or exploration. (Open science = open access + open process).

Platform: "All services and digital resources, uniquely accessible through a user name/password and where the presentation and organization varies in accordance with the user profile attributed to the user"[13]. A platform is a technical object accessible online, providing an integrated or connected set of services and resources, and intended for a particular section of the public.

Peer review: This refers to the validation of an article by a reading committee made up of scientists and experts in the same disciplinary field as the content of the article. This process is intended to ensure scientific quality[14].

Reader-payer: "The reader-payer model corresponds to the traditional publishing model, subscription. The reader can only have access to periodicals and works for a price, but this most often concerns his or her institution, with a subscription paid to one or several publishers. This is in opposition to the author-payer and sponsor-payer models"[15].

Semantic Web: Also known as the "data web", defined by Tim Berners-Lee as "a web of data which can be processed directly or indirectly by machines to help their users to create new knowledge". The Giant Global Graph (GGG) is a kind of semantic Web, with the addition of strong decentralization.

---

12 The vocabulary of information technology and JORF law no. 0103 of 3 May 2014, page 7639.
13 http://hal.archives-ouvertes.fr/docs/00/53/71/26/PDF/Cahier-Orme-1-Plates-formes-numeriques.pdf.
14 INIST glossary.
15 http://openaccess.inist.fr/spip.php?page=glossaire.

Shared asset: A non-rival asset, i.e. inexhaustible and which can be mobilized by an infinite number of people simultaneously and non-exclusively, as its immateriality seems at first sight to prevent its privatization.

Text and data mining (TDM): A method of automatic knowledge processing.

Bibliography

PART **1** – Production: Global Knowledge and Science in the Digital Era

Chapter 1. Current Knowledge Dynamics

COMETS (*Comité d'éthique du CNRS*), "Citizen Science", COMETS Position Paper, available at: http://www.cnrs.fr/comets/IMG/pdf/comets-avis-sciences_citoyennes-25_juin_2015_en-2.pdf, 25 June, 2015.

DIST (*Direction de l'Information Technique et Scientifique*), A better sharing of knowledge: An open policy for scientific and technical information of the future, CNRS, 2015.

Max Planck Society, Berlin Declaration on open access to knowledge in the sciences and humanities, available at: https://openaccess.mpg.de/Berlin-Declaration, October, 2003.

PATRICE F., *L'imaginaire d'Internet*, Editions de la Découverte, Paris, 2001.

Chapter 2. Digital Conditions for Knowledge Production

ARXIV, "General information about arXiv", available at: http://arxiv.org/help/general, accessed 2016.

BESTER E., "Les services pour les archives ouvertes: de la référence à l'expertise", *Documentaliste-Sciences de l'Information*, available at: www.cairn.info/revue-documentaliste-sciences-de-l-information-2010-4-page-4.htm, vol. 47, pp. 4–15, 2010.

DULONG DE ROSNAY M., "Les réseaux de production collaborative de connaissances", in LETONTURIER E. (ed.), *Les réseaux*, CNRS Editions, available at: https://hal.archives-ouvertes.fr/halshs-00726963v2/document/, pp. 141–146, 2012.

ÉRIC S., *La révolution numérique*, Dalloz, p. 224, 2009.

HEATON L., MILLERAND F., CRESPEL É. *et al.*, "La réactualisation de la contribution des amateurs à la botanique. Le collectif en ligne Tela Botanica", *Terrains & travaux*, available at: www.cairn.info/revue-terrains-et-travaux-2011-1-page-155.htm, no. 18, pp. 155–173, 2011.

JASON S., "Academic journals: the most profitable obsolete technology in history", The Huffington Post, available at: http://www.huffingtonpost.com/jason-schmitt/academic-journals-the-mos_1_b_6368204.html, 2015.

KAMIL I., "La propriété intellectuelle. Moteur de la croissance économique", Organisation Mondiale de la Propriété Intellectuelle (OMPI), available at: http://www. wipo.int/edocs/pubdocs/fr/intproperty/888/wipo_pub_888_1.pdf, June 2003.

LARIVIÈRE V., HAUSTEIN S., MONGEON P., "The oligopoly of academic publishers in the digital era", *PLoS One,* vol. 10, no. 6, p. e0127502, available at: http://127.0.0.1:8081/plosone/article?id=info:doi/10.1371/journal.pone.0127502, 2015.

LE CROSNIER H., "Culture numérique: 07 Wikipedia", video, available at: https://www.canal-u.tv/video/centre_d_enseignement_multimedia_universitaire_c_e_m_u/culture_numerique_07_wikipedia.8398, 2015.

LE CROSNIER H., "Culture numérique: 11 La propriété immatérielle", video, available at: https://www.canal-u.tv/video/centre_d_enseignement_multimedia_universitaire_c_e_m_u/culture_numerique_11_la_propriete_immaterielle.8403, 2015.

LE CROSNIER H., "Une bonne nouvelle pour la théorie des biens communs", *Vacarme*, available at: www.cairn.info/revue-vacarme-2011-3-page-92.htm, no. 56, pp. 92–94, 2011.

LE CROSNIER H., "Culture numérique: 12 Société de l'information, société de la connaissance", video, available at: https://www.canal-u.tv/video/centre_d_enseignement_multimedia_universitaire_c_e_m_u/culture_numerique_12_societe_de_l_information_societe_de_la_connaissance.8406, 2015.

PIERRE P., "Recherche scientifique", *Encyclopædia Universalis*, available at: https://www-universalis–edu-com.acces-distant.sciences-po.fr/encyclopedie/recherche-scientifique/, September 2015.

VALÉRIE P., "Les biens communs, une utopie pragmatique", VECAM, available at: http://vecam.org/archives/ article1304.html, September 2015.

WIKIPEDIA, "Creative Commons", available at: https://en.wikipedia.org/wiki/ Creative_Commons, accessed 2016.

WORLD BANK, "Charges for the use of intellectual property, payments (BoP, current US$)", available at: http://data.worldbank.org/indicator/BM.GSR.ROYL.CD, accessed 2016.

WORLD BANK, "Research and development expenditure (% of GDP)", available at: http://data.worldbank.org/indicator/GB.XPD.RSDV.GD.ZS, accessed 2016.

On the production of narrative knowledge:

PERAYA D., "Quel impact les technologies ont-elles sur la production et la diffusion des connaissances?", *Questions de communication*, available at: www.cairn.info/ revue-questions-de-communication-2012–page-89.htm, vol. 21, pp. 89–106, 2012

Chapter 3. The Dual Relationship between the User and the Developer

FAVIER L., EL HADI WIDAD M., "Introduction – L'archivage numérique des savoirs. Perspectives européennes", *Les Cahiers du numérique*, available at: www.cairn.info/revue-les-cahiers-du-numerique-2015-1-page-9.htm, vol. 11, pp. 9–14, 2015.

GUITTARD C., SCHENK E., BENGHOZI J-P. *et al.* (eds), "Knowledge management in society and organizations", *Management International*, vol. 16, pp. 1–143, 2012.

LIOTARD I., "Les plateformes d'innovation sur Internet: arrangements contractuels, intermédiation et gestion de la propriété intellectuelle", *Management International*, vol. 16, pp. 129–143, 2012

MATHIEU A. *et al.*, "Estimation des dépenses de publication de l'Inra dans un modèle théorique 'Gold Open Access'", *Documentaliste-Sciences de l'Information*, vol. 51, pp. 70–79, 2014.

Websites:

ISTEX – http://www.istex.fr/le-projet/.

Ministère de l'Enseignement Supérieur et de la Recherche (Ministry of Higher Education and Research) – http://www.enseignementsup-recherche.gouv.fr/ cid81329/signature-des-premiers-contrats-de-sites-issus-de-la-loi-relative-a-l-e.s.r. html

Cabinet Bastien – http://www.cabinetbastien.fr/publication-19022-les-enjeux-juridiques-du-crowdsourcing.html

Chapter 4. Researchers' Uses and Needs for Scientific and Technical Information

Agence d'Evaluation de la Recherche et de l'Enseignement Supérieur (Agency for the Evaluation of Higher Education and Research) – http://www.aeres-evaluation.fr/

Centre National de la Recherche Scientifique – http://www.cnrs.fr/

DBLP – http://dblp.uni-trier.de/

Hal – https://hal.archives-ouvertes.fr/

Ministère de l'Enseignement Supérieur et de la Recherche (Ministry of Higher Education and Research) – http://www. enseignementsup-recherche.gouv.fr/

Publications – Coline Ferrant – https://colineferrant.wordpress.com/publications/

ResearchGate – https://www.researchgate.net/

Réseau National des Bibliothèques de Mathématiques (National Network of Mathematical Libraries) – http://www.rnbm.org/

Chapter 6. Modes of Knowledge Sharing and Technologies

DIST *(La Direction de l'information scientifique et technique* – Directorate of Scientific and Technical Information) – CNRS – http://www.cnrs.fr/dist/

INIST – http://www.inist.fr

INRIA – http://www.inria.fr

INRIA YouTube Channel – https://www.youtube.com/user/InriaChannel

PART 2 – Sharing Mechanisms: Knowledge Sharing and the Knowledge-based Economy

Chapter 7. Business Model for Scientific Publication

BADEN-FULLER C., HAEFLIGER S., "Business models and technological innovation", *Long Range Planning*, vol. 46, pp. 419–426, 2013.

BERNARD G., PIERRE D., RODOLPHE D., *Strategor: Toute la stratégie d'entreprise*, Dunod, 2009.

PERRY N., "Publications scientifique en Open Access", video, available at: https://www.canal-u.tv/video/universite_bordeaux_segalen_dcam/embed.1/publication_en_%20open_access_temoignage.16349?width=100%&height=100%, 2015.

PERRY N., "Un témoignage de l'intérêt du libre accès", video, available at: http://guide-hal.univ-grenoble-alpes.fr/fr/la-veille/blog/un-temoignage-de-l-interet-du-libre-acces-par-nicolas-perry-enseignant-chercheur-cnam-campus-de-bordeaux--636957.htm, 2014.

Chapter 8. Actor Strategy: International Scientific Publishing, Services with High Added Value and Research Communities

BACH J-F., JÉROME D., Les nouveaux enjeux de l'édition scientifique, Report, l'Académie des sciences, 2014.

BOURDIEU P., "Une révolution conservatrice dans l'édition", *Actes de la recherche en sciences sociales*, vol. 126, 1999.

CARDON D., *A quoi rêvent les algorithmes. Nos vies à l'heure des big data*, Seuil, 2015.

CNRS, L'édition de sciences à l'heure du numérique, Report, 2015.

DIST (*Direction de l'Information Technique et Scientifique*), A better sharing of knowledge: An open policy for scientific and technical information of the future, CNRS, 2015.

FLOCH B., "Deux sociologues piègent une revue pour dénoncer la 'junk science'", Le Monde, available at: http://www.lemonde.fr/education/article/2015/03/10/la-revue-societes-piegee-par-deux-sociologues_4590914_1473685.html, 10th March, 2015.

GINGRAS Y., *Les dérives de l'évaluation de la recherche. Du bon usage de la bibliométrie*, Raisons d'agir, 2014.

VAJOU M. "Les enjeux économiques de l'édition scientifique, technique et médicale", *Les cahiers du numérique*, vol. 5, 2009.

Websites:

Educpros – educpros.fr

CNRS – cnrs.fr

Chapter 9. New Approaches to Scientific Production

On the opening up of the scientific evaluation process:

DEVILLE S., "Articles bidons dans les revues: non, ce n'est pas la faute à l'Open Access", available at: http://rue89.nouvelobs.com/2013/10/05/articles-bidons-les-revues-non-nest-faute-a-lopen-access-24632, 2013.

RICE C., "What *Science* – and the Gonzo Scientist – got wrong: open access will make research better", available at: http://curt-rice.com/2013/10/04/what-science-and-the-gonzo-scientist-got-wrong-open-access-will-make-research-better/, 2013.

VELTEROP J., "Essence of academic publishing", available at: http://theparachute. blogspot.co.uk/2013/11/essence-of-academic-publishing.html, 2013.

On overlay journals:

BERTHAUD C., CAPELLI L., GUSTEDT J. *et al.*, "EPISCIENCES – an overlay publication platform", *ELPUB2014 – International Conference on Electronic Publishing*, Thessalonique, Greece, available at: https://hal.inria.fr/hal-0100 2815, pp. 78–87, 2014.

DIST (*Direction de l'Information Technique et Scientifique*), Dynamiques de l'édition scientifique, de l'industrie, de l'information, de la documentation, Report, CNRS, available at: http://www.cnrs.fr/dist/z-outils/documents/ actescolloquesdessids.pdf, 2014.

GOWERS T., "Why I've also joined the good guys", available at: https://gowers. wordpress.com/2013/01/16/why-ive-also-joined-the-good-guys/, 2013.

VAN NOORDEN R., "Mathematicians aim to take publishers out of publishing", available at: http://www.nature.com/news/mathematicians-aim-to-take-publishers-out-of-publishing-1.12243, 2013.

On megajournals:

DIST (*Direction de l'Information Technique et Scientifique*), Les éditeurs scientifiques "for profit" accélèrent leur conversion à l'Open Access Gold: quelles visées stratégiques sous-jacentes?, Report, CNRS, available at: http://www.cnrs.fr/dist/z-outils/documents/Distinfo2/Distinf8.pdf, 2015.

DIST (*Direction de l'Information Technique et Scientifique*), Elsevier lance sa méga-revue multidisciplinaire Heliyon, Report, CNRS, available at: http://www.cnrs.fr/dist/z-outils/documents/Distinfo2/Distinfo16.pdf, 2015.

On the "digital halo" of scientific and technical information:

DIST (*Direction de l'Information Technique et Scientifique*), La publication scientifique aujourd'hui: financement, usages numériques, Study, available at: http://www.cnrs.fr/dist/z-outils/documents/Distinfo2/DISTetude_4.pdf, 2015.

NASSI-CALÒ L., "Unpublished results from clinical trials distort medical research", available at: http://blog.scielo.org/en/2015/08/12/unpublished-results-from-clinical-trials-distort-medical-research/, 2015.

On bibliometric indicators:

FABRE R., "Les indicateurs bibliométriques de l'IST et l'Innovation: Que peut-on mesurer aujourd'hui?", DIST (CNRS), available at: http://www.cnrs.fr/dist/z-outils/documents/indicateurs%20bibliometriques%20Innovation_8sept2014.pdf, 2014.

On academic social networks:

BENECH C., "Protection et propriété des données sur Academia.edu et ResearchGate", available at: http://archeorient.hypotheses.org/2554, 2014.

BOUCHARD A., "Pour une utilisation critique des réseaux sociaux académiques", available at: http://urfistinfo.hypotheses.org/2596, 2014.

BOUCHARD A., "Où en est-on des réseaux sociaux académiques?", available at: http://urfistinfo.hypotheses.org/2896, 2015.

Chapter 10. The Geopolitics of Science

ANDRÉ F., *Libre accès aux savoirs*, Futuribles 2005.

AZÉMA J., EDELMAN B., VIVANT M., "Brevet d'invention", *Encyclopaedia Universalis*, available at: http://www.universalis.fr/encyclopedie/brevet-d-invention/, accessed 2016.

BAQUIAST J-P., "Puissance scientifique: Chine, Etats-Unis, Europe: La Chine dépassera-t-elle les Etats-Unis?", available at: http://www.automatesintelligents. com/echanges/2014/fev/puissance_chine_usa_europe.html, 2014.

COSTE J-H., "La dynamique de la recherche et développement aux Etats-Unis: origines et évolution du système d'innovation américain", *Revue LISA*, vol. IV, pp. 10–28, available at: https://lisa.revues.org/2117, 2006.

EUROPEAN UNION, Strategeic framework for the international scientific and technological cooperation, Communcation no. COM(2008) 588, available at: http://eur-lex.europa.eu/legal-content/FR/TXT/?uri=uriserv:ri0006, 2008.

FRANCIS A., Les enjeux autour des données de la recherche, available at: http://renatis.cnrs.fr/IMG/pdf/fANDRE_AUSSOIS_FREDOC2013.pdf, 2013.

HUET S., "Le bond en avant de la science en Chine", available at: http://sciences.blogs.liberation.fr/home/2013/06/le-bond-en-avant-de-la-science-enchine.html, 2013.

MAX PLANCK SOCIETY, Berlin Declaration on open access to knowledge in the sciences and humanities, available at: https://openaccess.mpg.de/Berlin-Declaration, October, 2003.

MURRAY-RUST P., NEYLON C., POLLOCK R. *et al.*, "Panton Principles", available at: http://pantonprinciples.org, 2010.

WORLD INTELLECTUAL PROPERTY ORGANIZATION (WIPO), Managing IP at CERN, *WIPO Magazine*, available at: http://www.wipo.int/ wipo_magazine/en/2010/06/article_0003.html, vol. 2010, no. 6, 2010.

Websites:

CNRS, Espace Européen de la Recherche, available at: http://www.cnrs.fr/derci/spip.php?article15, accessed 2016.

CORDIS (Community Research and Development Information Service): http://cordis.europa.eu/home_fr.html

COST (European Cooperation in Science and Technology): http://www.cost.eu/about_cost/strategy

Creative Commons articles on CERN: http://creativecommons.org/tag/cern

Articles from the Ministère de l'Enseignement Supérieur et de la Recherche (Ministry of Higher Education and Research):

La politique de coopération internationale: http://www.enseignementsup-recherche.gouv.fr/cid56277/la-politique-de-cooperationinternationale.html

Politique de coopération multilatérale: http://www.enseignementsup-recherche.gouv.fr/cid56280/la-cooperation-multilaterale.html

Espace Européen de la Recherche: http://www.enseignementsup-recherche.gouv.fr/cid56014/presentation-de-l-e.e.r.html

Dimension internationale de l'EER: http://www.horizon2020.gouv.fr/ cid74231/dimension-internationale-espace-europeenrecherche.html

Bulletin des Bibliothèques de France, "Nouveaux Outils de la connaissance et partage des savoirs", André Garcia, 2007: http://www.horizon2020.gouv.fr/cid 74231/dimension-internationale-espace-europeenrecherche.html

Articles from the OECD (Organisation for Economic Co-operation and Development):

OECD, Mesurer la mondialisation: Indicateurs de l'OCDE sur la mondialisation économique, OECD Publishing, 2006.

OECD, Principles and guidelines for access to research data from public funding, available at: http://www.oecd.org/sti/sci-tech/38500813.pdf, 2007.

OECD, Compendium of Patent Statistics 2008, Report, available at: http://www.oecd.org/sti/inno/37569377.pdf, 2008.

OECD, "China headed to overtake EU, US in science & technology spending, OECD says", available at: http://www.oecd.org/newsroom/china-headed-to-overtake-eu-us-in-science-technology-spending.htm, 2014.

OECD, "International cooperation in patents", available at: http://stats.oecd.org/Index.aspx?DatasetCode=PATS_COOP, 2015.

OECD, Main science and technology indicators, vol. 2016, no.1, available at: http://www.oecd-ilibrary.org/docserver/download/9414012e.pdf?expires=14424 94532&id=id&accname=ocid195751&checksum=B1042F89A5DB638D1895C 069FA08FC25, 2016.

OECD, Travaux de l'OCDE sur les statistiques de brevets, available at: http://www.oecd.org/fr/innovation/inno/travauxdelocdesurlesstatistiquesdebrevets, accessed 2016.

OECD, Open Science policy trends, available at: http://www.oecd.org/ sti/outlook/eoutlook/stipolicyprofiles/interactionsforinnovation/openscience, accessed 2016.

OECD, Forum mondial de la science de l'OCDE, available at: http://www.oecd. org/fr/sti/sci-tech/forummondialdelasciencedelocde, accessed 2016.

OECD, Bases de données de brevets de l'OCDE, available at: http:// www.oecd.org/ fr/sti/inno/basesdedonneesdebrevetsdelocde, accessed 2016.

OECD, Principaux indicateurs de la science et de la technologie, available at: http://www.oecd.org/fr/sti/pist, accessed 2016.

PART 3 – Enhancement Knowledge Rights and Public Policies in the Wake of Digital Technology

Chapter 12. Legal Protection of Scientific Research Results in the Humanities and Social Sciences

BONNET Y., "Tribune: Favoriser la libre diffusion de la culture et des savoirs", http://www.cnnumerique.fr/communs/, 2015.

DELMAS C., Droit, éthique et sciences sociales", *Espaces Temps*, available at: http://www.espacestemps.net/articles/droit-ethique-et-sciences-sociales, 2011.

OECD, "Legal aspects of open access to publicly funded research", in "Enquiries into intellectual property's economic impact", OECD Report, available at: http://www.oecd.org/sti/ieconomy/Chapter7-KBC2-IP.pdf, 2015.

OURAL M., "Gouvernance des Politiques Numériques dans les Territoires", Report, Pôle Numérique, available at: http://www.pole-numerique.fr/images/documents/ Gouvernance_numerique_rapport AkimOural.pdf

SYLVAIN L., FRÉDÉRIC N. (eds), *Enquêter: de quel droit? Menaces sur l'enquête en sciences sociales*, Éd. du Croquant, 2010.

Websites:

Conseil supérieur de la propriété littéraire et artistique, "La protection par le droit d'auteur": http://www.culture.gouv.fr/culture/infospratiques/droits/protection. htm

Creative Commons France, "6 Licences Gratuites": http://creativecommons.fr/ licences

DIST (*Direction de l'Information Technique et Scientifique*), "Le brevet d'invention": http://www.cnrs.fr/dire/termes_cles/brevet.htm

Droit & Technologies, Validité des Creative Commons face au droit français: http:// www.droit-technologie.org/dossier-186/validite-des-creative-commons-face-au- droit-francais.html

HAL open archive, "Creative Commons licenses": https://hal.archives-ouvertes.fr/page/questions-juridiques#licences_cc

INPI, La solution de l'enveloppe Soleau: http://www.inpi.fr/fr/enveloppes-soleau.html

Le Monde, "Favorisons la libre diffusion de la culture et des savoirs": www.lemonde.fr/idees/article/2015/09/10/favorisons-la-libre-diffusion-de-la-culture-et-des-savoirs_4751847_3232.html

Manitoba Government, Manitoba Curriculum Framework of Outcomes: http://www.edu.gov.mb.ca/m12/frpub/ped/sh/cadre-m-9/index.html

Chapter 13. Development of Knowledge and Public Policies

BIMBOT R., MARTELLY I., "La recherche fondamentale, source de tout progrès", available at: http://histoire-cnrs.revues.org/9141, 2009.

CGEDD, "Valorisation de la Recherche, brevets et propriété intellectuelle : c'était le 27 janvier 2010", http://www.cgedd.developpement-durable.gouv.fr/valorisation-de-la-recherche-brevets-et-propriete-a525.html

CNRS, "Innovatives SHS, le premier salon de la valorisation en sciences humaines et socials": http://www2.cnrs.fr/presse/communique/3043.htm

Institut des Hautes Etudes pour la Science et la Technologie, "L'innovation aux Etats-Unis": http://www.ihest.fr/IMG/article_PDF/ article_a862.pdf

Les-aides, "Les aides pour l'innovation": https://les-aides.fr/focus/bZBk/les-aides-pour-l-innovation.html

Chapter 14. From Author to Enhancer

BRESSE P., "Valorisation des connaissances et marchandisation des savoirs", in LUCAS D., MOINET N. (eds), Géoéconomie, Editions Choiseul, 2010

CAPACITÉS, "CAPACITÉS, filiale de valorisation de la recherche de l'Université de Nantes", video, https://www.youtube.com/watch?v=lelfiJDdMeQ, 2015.

Conseil de la Science et de la Technologie du Québec, Chaînes de valorisation de résultats de la recherche universitaire recelant un potentiel d'utilisation par une entreprise ou par un autre milieu, Report, Québec, 2006.

CNRS, "Service Partenariat et Valorisation – Industrie", available at: http://www.cnrs.fr/midi-pyrenees/AVotreService/PV/Industrie/TypoContrats.aspx

MENDES P., "Concession de licences et transfert de technologie", Report, OMPI, available at: http://www.wipo.int/sme/fr/ documents/pharma_licensing.html, 2006.

SÉNAT, L'Agence nationale de valorisation de la recherche (ANVAR): une gestion à l'envers, Report no. 220, available at: http://www.senat.fr/rap/r06-220/r06-2209.html, 2007.

WIKIPÉDIA "Valorisation de la recherche", https://fr.wikipedia.org/wiki/Valorisation_de_la_recherche, accessed 2016

Chapter 15. The Right to Knowledge – Moving Towards a Universal Law?

INSTITUT FRANÇAIS DES RELATIONS INTERNATIONALES (ed.), "Internet: une gouvernance inachevée", *Politique etrangère*, 4/2014, 2015.

JURCYS P., KJAER P.F., YATSUNAMI R. (eds), *Regulatory Hybridization in the Transnational Sphere*, Martinus Nijhoff Publishers, 2013.

KAHIN B., NESSON C. (eds), *Borders in Cyberspace, Information Policy and the Global Information Infrastructure*, MIT Press, 1997.

KULESZA J., *International Internet Law*, Routledge, London, New York, 2012.

LESSIG L., "Code is law", *Harvard Magazine*, available at: http://harvardmagazine.com/2000/01/code-is-law-html, 2000.

PRICE M.E., "Ghosts, vampires and the global shaping of Internet policy", in BECK R.J., *Law and Disciplinarity: Thinking Beyond Borders*, Palgrave Macmillan, 2013.

ZIMMER M., "Internet privacy across borders: 'trading up' or a 'race to the bottom'?", in BECK R.J. (ed.), *Law and Disciplinarity: Thinking Beyond Borders*, Palgrave Macmillan, 2013.

Websites:

"Comment ça marche Internet?", article, available at: http://www.culture-informatique.net/comment-ca-marche-internet/, 2014.

CISAC (International Confederation of Societies of Authors and Composers), http:// www.cisac.org/

European Union, La Commission ouvre une procédure concernant l'octroi de licences sur les droits d'auteur musicaux pour utilisation sur Internet, europa.eu/rapid/press-release_IP-04-586_fr.pdf, Report no. IP/04/586, 2004.

ICANN (Internet Corporation for Assigned Names and Numbers): www.icann.org/

IWG (International Working Group of Sovereign Wealth Funds): "Principes de Santiago", www.iwg-swf.org/pubs/fra/gapplistf.pdf

European Commission, "Santiago Agreement Potentially Incompatible with European Competition Law", available at http://merlin.obs.coe.int/iris/2004/6/article9.fr.html

Le Monde, "Oui, Internet est un " bien public", available at http www.lemonde.fr/idees/ article/2015/02/ 27/oui-internet-est-un-bien-public_4584618_3232.html

World Summit on the Information Society 2005, http://www. itu.int/net/wsis/wgig/

WSIS Forum 2015, "Innovating together, enabling ICTs for sustainable development", http://www.itu.int/net4/wsis/forum/2015/

Chapter 16. Governing by Algorithm

ALAIN D., *La Politique des grands nombres: Histoire de la raison statistique*, 2nd ed., La Découverte, Paris, 2000.

ALAIN S., *La Gouvernance par les nombres*, Fayard, Paris, 2015.

EDEN M., *Cybernetic Revolutionaries*, The MIT Press, Boston, 2014.

ÉMILIEN R., Trop de fonctionnaires? Contribution à une histoire de l'État par ses effectifs (France, 1850–1950), PhD Thesis, Ecole des Hautes Etudes en Sciences Sociales, 2013.

EVGENY M., *Pour tout résoudre cliquez ici*, FYP Editions, 2014.

HENRI V., NICOLAS C., *L'âge de la multitude: Entreprendre et gouverner après la révolution numérique*, Armand Collin, Paris, 2012.

KHANNA P., KHANNA A., *Hybrid Reality: Thriving in the Emerging Human-Technology Civilization*, TED Books, 2012.

O REILEY T., *Beyond Transparency*, Code For America Press, 2013.

Chapter 17. Public Data and Science in e-Government

http://www.cpu.fr/actualite/les-donnees-de-la-science-un-bien-commun/

http://www.republique-numerique.fr/project/projet-de-loi-numerique/step/projet-de-loi-adopte-par-le-conseil-des-ministres

https://www.actualitte.com/article/monde-edition/le-projet-istex-pour-renforcer-la-recherche-francaise/35817

http://www.data-publica.com/content/2012/09/donnees-publiques-payantes-les-points-de-vue-de-simon-chignard-et-de-regards-citoyens/

http://www.modernisation.gouv.fr/laction-publique-se-transforme/en-ouvrant-les-don nees-publiques/administrateur-general-des-donnees-chief-data-officer-interview-henri-verdier

http://abonnes.lemonde.fr/technologies/chat/2010/06/30/a-quoi-servent-les-donnees-publiques_1381218_651865.html

http://www.lagazettedescommunes.com/377609/donnees-publiques-lechelle-des-priorites/

http://www.internetactu.net/2010/11/09/louverture-des-donnees-publiques-et-apres/

http://www.zdnet.fr/actualites/open-data-liberons-toutes-les-donnees-publiques-et-dans-de-bonnes-conditions-de-reutilisabilite-39800441.htm

Chapter 18. Surveillance, *Sousveillance*, Improper Capturing

BENTHAM J., *Panoptique: mémoire sur un nouveau principe pour construire des maisons d'inspection, et nommément des maisons de force*, Hachette, 2012.

BERNAULT C., "Revues scientifiques et droit d'auteur: la rupture de l'open access", *Hermès, La Revue*, no. 71, C.N.R.S. Editions, 2015.

FAYET S., "Open access et droit d'auteur", in MALKA R. (ed.), *La gratuité, c'est le vol. 2015: la fin du droit d'auteur?*, Editions Richard, 2015.

GANASCIA J.-G., *Voir et pouvoir: qui nous surveille?*, Le Pommier, Paris, 2009.

QUESSADA D., "De la sousveillance", *Multitudes*, no. 40, pp. 54–59, 2010.

Websites:

http://www.cnrs.fr/comitenational/doc/recommandations/2015/Reco_Projet_de_loi_sur_le_numerique_24-25_sept_15.pdf

http://www.cnrs.fr/dist/z-outils/documents/Distinfo2/Distinf14.pdf

http://www2.deloitte.com/us/en/pages/technology/articles/tech-trends-2015-api-economy-report.html

http://www.alain-bensoussan.com/wp-content/uploads/2015/07/22684756.pdf

http://www.alain-bensoussan.com/wp-content/uploads/2014/05/28131372.pdf

http://www.republique-numerique.fr/projects/projet-de-loi-numerique/consultation/consultation/opinions/section-3-loyaute-des-plateformes/normalisation-des-application-programming-interfaces-api-interfaces-de-programmation

Chapter 19. Public Knowledge Policies in the Digital Age

BERNE X., La nouvelle version de l'avant-projet de loi numérique d'Axelle Lemaire, Nextimpact, available at: http://www.nextinpact.com/news/96384-la-nouvelle-version-avant-projet-loi-numerique-daxelle-lemaire.htm, 2015.

Chaire Innovation & Régulation des Services Numériques, Compte rendu de la conférence – La Régulation des Plateformes Numériques, available at: http://innovation-regulation2.telecom-paristech.fr/wp-content/uploads/2015/06/La-R%C3%A9gulation-des-Plateformes-Num%C3%A9riques-CR-Defdef.pdf, 2015.

COLLECTIF, Favorisons la libre diffusion de la culture et des savoirs, Le Monde, http://www.lemonde.fr/idees/article/2015/09/10/favorisons-la-libre-diffusion-de-la-culture-et-des-savoirs_4751847_3232.html, 2015.

CONSEIL NATIONAL DU NUMÉRIQUE, Rapport sur la neutralité des plateformes, Report, available at: http://www.cnnumerique.fr/wp-content/uploads/2014/06/CNNum_Rapport_Neutralite_des_plateformes.pdf, 2014.

CONSEIL NATIONAL DU NUMÉRIQUE, Neutralité des plateformes. Compte-rendu du 2ème vendredi contributif, Report, available at: http://www.cnnumerique.fr/wp-content/uploads/2013/11/CRVC_10.10_PDFTOWORD.pdf, 2013.

CONSEIL NATIONAL DU NUMÉRIQUE, Neutralité des plateformes – compte rendu du 3ème vendredi contributif, Report, available at: http://www.cnnumerique.fr/wp-content/uploads/2013/11/Plateformes_CRVC_8.11_V1JHBCMBrevuBensoussan.pdf, 2013.

CNIL, Sanctions prononcées depuis l'entrée en vigueur de la loi relative au défenseur des droits, http://www.cnil.fr/linstitution/missions/sanctionner/les-sanctions-prononcees-par-la-cnil/, accessed 2016.

DOUGHERTY C., F.T.C. is said to investigate claims that Google used Android to promote its products, New York Times, available at: http://www.nytimes.com/2015/09/26/technology/ftc-is-said-to-investigate-claims-that-google-used-android-to-promote-its-products.html?_r=0, 2015.

GUITON A., La "République numérique» dans le texte, Libération, http://www.liberation.fr/economie/2015/09/26/la-republique-numerique-a-l-heure-du-changement_1391110, 2015.

LA RÉPUBLIQUE NUMÉRIQUE EN ACTES, https://www.republique-numerique.fr, accessed 2016.

PENARD T., MAXWELL W., Réguler les plateformes: une fausse bonne idée, L'Opinion, http://www.lopinion.fr/23-avril-2015/reguler-plateformes-fausse-bonne-idee-23627, 2015.

Chapter 20. The Politics of Creating Artificial Intelligence

AMAR M., MENON B., "Semantic web, data web: What is the new deal?", *Documentaliste Sciences de l'Information*, vol. 48, no. 4, 2011.

AUGUSTIN H., JEAN-MICHEL H., "L'intelligence artificielle au service du marketing", *L'Expansion Management Review*, no. 146, 2012.

DANIÈLE B., "De l'intelligence artificielle à la personne virtuelle: émergence d'une entité juridique?", *Droit et société,* no. 49, 2001.

ERIC S., *La Société de l'anticipation*, Editions Inculte, Paris, 2011.

La République numérique en actes, "Project de loi pour une République numérique", http://www.republique-numerique.fr/projects/projet-de-loi-numerique/consultation/consultation/opinions/section-3-loyaute-des-plateformes/donner-la-priorite-aux-logiciels-libres-et-aux-formats-ouverts-dans-le-service-public-national-et-local, 2015.

RUSS A., "Distribute AI benefits fairly", *Nature*, vol. 521, 2015.

Index

A, B

allègre act, 115
american model, 80
API, 140, 144
archives, 8, 9, 11, 12, 17, 24, 34, 44,
    63, 68, 69, 73, 79, 139, 178, 179
article processing charge, 51, 83, 177
artificial intelligence, 157, 177
authors' rights, 87
automation, 128–130
big deal, 50
business model, 49

C, D

CERN, 81
certification, 67, 69, 145
China, 11, 12, 16, 60, 80, 85, 86, 122,
    123
CNRS, 94, 95
common market, 25
commons, 13–14
community, 25
consultation services, 63
copyright, 85
creative commons, 24, 52, 82, 96, 99,
    144, 178

crowd
    funding, 26
    sourcing, 18, 26, 178
data
    management, 33
    web, 180
database, 8, 18, 33–35, 43, 44, 135,
    136, 139, 144, 169, 178, 179
digital
    halo, 49, 52–54
    republic, 124, 138

E, F

economic models, 145, 146
editors, 93
EPIC, 79
episciences, 69
EPST, 79
ERA-NET, 109
Etalab project, 131, 137
European Union, 7, 51, 81–83, 87,
    106, 107, 109, 110
financing, 26, 33, 49–51, 79, 82, 108,
    110, 115, 178
freedom, 119, 131, 166–168

G, H, I, J

gold open access, 24, 25
green open access, 24
hard sciences, 91, 92, 94, 105
impact, 21, 59, 62, 63, 73, 74, 99,
    121, 123, 127, 129, 130
INPI, 97, 98, 106
intellectual ownership, 94
invention, 85, 87, 94, 112–114, 116
journal, 8, 68–71, 93, 178
junk science, 57

K, L, M, N

knowledge sharing, 43
lost science, 52, 53, 72, 73, 179
margin, 60
metadata, 37–40, 83, 155, 171–173,
    179
monopoly, 62, 63, 85, 151, 153, 155
nanotechnology, 110

O, P

open
    archive, 5, 8, 21, 24, 63, 68, 69, 75,
        178, 179
    process, 51, 52, 131, 180
    science, 6, 22, 63, 64, 81, 134, 139,
        143–147
organic-digital, 166
participative science, 4
patent, 1–6, 13, 21, 34, 77, 83–85, 92,
    105, 113, 179

peer review

peer review, 15, 49, 53, 60, 68, 70,
    71, 83, 93, 99, 178, 180
plagiarism, 8, 53, 71, 98, 144
pre-print, 68, 69
privacy, 136, 161
private publisher, 49–51
profitability, 49, 57, 61, 62

R, S

references, 20, 44, 73, 127
research services, 63
royalty, 16, 21, 85, 86
self-regulation, 17, 126
semantic web, 38–41, 180
silicon valley, 78, 108, 109
smart content, 158, 160, 161
social network, 15, 16, 37, 64, 71–75,
    145
Soleau envelope, 97
start-up, 109, 115, 135, 151
storage, 4, 8, 43, 44, 133, 159
strategies, 50, 58, 59, 63, 64, 113

T, V, W

targeting, 37
text mining, 40, 51
transhumanism, 158
transparency, 4–9, 53, 68–71, 136–
    138, 155
visibility, 59, 60, 74, 75, 105, 151
wealth distribution, 51

Other titles from

in

Cognitive Science and Knowledge Management

2016

CLERC Maureen, BOUGRAIN Laurent, LOTTE Fabien
Brain–Computer Interfaces 1: Foundations and Methods
Brain–Computer Interfaces 2: Technology and Applications

FORT Karën
Collaborative Annotation for Reliable Natural Language Processing

GIANNI Robert
Responsibility and Freedom
(Responsible Research and Innovation Set – Volume 2)

KURDI Mohamed Zakaria
Natural Language Processing and Computational Linguistics 1: Speech,
Morphology and Syntax

LENOIR Virgil Cristian
Ethical Efficiency: Responsibility and Contingency
(Responsible Research and Innovation Set – Volume 1)

MATTA Nada, ATIFI Hassan, DUCELLIER Guillaume
Daily Knowledge Valuation in Organizations

NOUVEL Damien, EHRMANN Maud, ROSSET Sophie
Named Entities for Computational Linguistics

PELLÉ Sophie, REBER Bernard
From Ethical Review to Responsible Research and Innovation (Responsible Research and Innovation Set - Volume 3)

REBER Bernard
Precautionary Principle, Pluralism and Deliberation (Responsible Research and Innovation Set – Volume 4)

SILBERZTEIN Max
Formalizing Natural Languages: The NooJ Approach

2015

LAFOURCADE Mathieu, JOUBERT Alain, LE BRUN Nathalie
Games with a Purpose (GWAPs)

SAAD Inès, ROSENTHAL-SABROUX Camille, GARGOURI Faïez
Information Systems for Knowledge Management

2014

DELPECH Estelle Maryline
Comparable Corpora and Computer-assisted Translation

FARINAS DEL CERRO Luis, INOUE Katsumi
Logical Modeling of Biological Systems

MACHADO Carolina, DAVIM J. Paulo
Transfer and Management of Knowledge

TORRES-MORENO Juan-Manuel
Automatic Text Summarization

2013

TURENNE Nicolas
Knowledge Needs and Information Extraction: Towards an Artificial Consciousness

ZARATÉ Pascale
Tools for Collaborative Decision-Making

2011

DAVID Amos
Competitive Intelligence and Decision Problems

LÉVY Pierre
The Semantic Sphere: Computation, Cognition and Information Economy

LIGOZAT Gérard
Qualitative Spatial and Temporal Reasoning

PELACHAUD Catherine
Emotion-oriented Systems

QUONIAM Luc
Competitive Intelligence 2.0: Organization, Innovation and Territory

2010

ALBALATE Amparo, MINKER Wolfgang
Semi-Supervised and Unsupervised Machine Learning: Novel Strategies

BROSSAUD Claire, REBER Bernard
Digital Cognitive Technologies

2009

BOUYSSOU Denis, DUBOIS Didier, PIRLOT Marc, PRADE Henri
Decision-making Process

MARCHAL Alain
From Speech Physiology to Linguistic Phonetics

PRALET Cédric, SCHIEX Thomas, VERFAILLIE Gérard
Sequential Decision-Making Problems / Representation and Solution

SZÜCS Andras, TAIT Alan, VIDAL Martine, BERNATH Ulrich
Distance and E-learning in Transition

2008

MARIANI Joseph
Spoken Language Processing

Printed and bound by CPI Group (UK) Ltd, Croydon, CR0 4YY

27/10/2024

14580237-0002